WAS

The Principles and Practice of
Youth and Community Work

The Principles and Practice of Youth and Community Work

by

J. P. Leighton

Senior Lecturer, Department of
Community and Youth work – Leicester
College of Education

Chester House Publications
2, Chester House, Pages Lane, London N10 1PZ

First published January 1972

ISBN 0 7150 0047 0

Printed in Great Britain by
Cox and Wyman Ltd,
London, Reading and Fakenham

CONTENTS

PREFACE

The changing youth scene reflected in the Youth Service as in other areas of life and work has for some time highlighted the need for a new text book to match the fresh approach and new methods in our training work.

The terms of reference acknowledge the specific requirements not only of the MAYC Basic Certificate Course but also the wider scope of our programme of training. Mr. Leighton's book is intended to provide a basis of training for those who want an understanding of what youth work is about and to study seriously the essentials of the subject.

BILL COCKELL

ACKNOWLEDGEMENTS

I am indebted to the Reverend Douglas S. Hubery not only for the Foreword which he has so kindly added to the book but for his comments on the proposed framework and continued encouragement during the subsequent writing. My thanks are extended to the Reverend George Cloke for framing the questions at the end of the book and together with Bill Cockell and Islwyn Jones for their invaluable help while the book was in draft form; to the typists in the Youth and Community Service of the Methodist Youth Department who struggled with my manuscripts and to innumerable people who have provided material without which the book could not have been written.

J. P. LEIGHTON

FOREWORD

by D. S. Hubery

It is no accident that the Service of Youth in England and Wales in terms of partnership between the state and voluntary organizations was established at the same time as the compulsory religious clauses of a new Education Act were accepted by both state and church. In their different ways, the concern that boys and girls in their formative years and young people who had left school and had time on their hands should find a satisfying way of life in terms of spiritual or Christian fulfilment was widely acknowledged. The fearful consequences of a generation that could be won over to a Fascist or Nazi philosophy of life, and the demoralizing influences of war-time conditions, in the modern world, were only too apparent. In both formal and informal sectors of education there was a tacit acceptance of the view that a growing generation should be given a full opportunity of coming to understand and to respond to a spiritual interpretation of life, and for the overwhelming majority this was interpreted as a process of Christian education.

The situation today is very different. The validity of the Christian faith is much more open to question by increasing numbers of people, and there are those who now speak of the post-Christian era on the assumption that whatever may have been useful in the past emanating from the Christian religion, it is no longer either desirable or necessary or acceptable. We live in a pluralistic and permissive society reflecting many religious cultures and even more varieties of accepted standards and values. And all this has inevitably affected our understanding of what education is, or ought to be, and, therefore, our attitude towards Christian education itself. Only in this context can we see what is the proper place of a Youth and Community Service and the ways in which Christians and the Christian Church can continue to play their part in that Service. It is always easy to speak with hindsight; but the truth of the matter is that the Service of Youth ought never to have been regarded as a means of making Christians, and doing the work which properly belongs to the Church itself. Only now are we beginning to recognize that education is rightly concerned with bringing understanding to life – even an understanding of the place which the Christian religion still has in life – but that to expect it to do more is to remove it from the realms of education as such.

The function of bringing understanding to life involves not only an awareness of all that has led society to become what it is, with its particular public institutions and accepted practices and symbols, but also a critical appraisal of these facets of life. From an educational point of view, as well as from a true radical Christian point of view, we ought not to be surprised if we find ourselves dealing with a generation extremely critical of 'the establishment' in Church and state and ready to express their disapproval in ways which twenty years ago would have been quite unthinkable.

All who are involved in working with young people today, whether as professionals or as voluntary workers, are facing tremendous challenges in seeking honestly to meet the needs of their constituency and so to interpret life that the modern generation may express its criticism creatively and positively for the benefit of community life as it will unfold in the next twenty years. And they need all the support and encouragement they can find.

For this reason I hope that Mr. Leighton's book will be read by all who are involved in any way in Youth and Community development; teachers and educators; ministers of religion and church leaders. In particular I hope his chapters which deal with Purpose and Principles will be studied with the greatest care. Those who are most anxious about the participation of the Churches in Youth work need to become much more clear than in the past about the aims and goals they set themselves, and their relation to legitimate processes of education as this is outlined in these two chapters.

The more I myself have sought to study the life of Jesus as a Teacher the more convinced I have become that he recognized a distinction between education and instruction, even if in those days precision of definition of abstract terms was unknown. There is a marked difference between his 'open-ended', undirected concept of teaching which he offered to the crowds, the general public, the people who for one reason or another came into contact with him; and the more specific and directed instruction he was able to offer to those who committed themselves to follow him. Church Youth Work, in so far as it is an expression of partnership with the state in the informal sector of education, should similarly be open-ended and undirected. It must certainly be free from any charge of indoctrination by whatever subtle process. And this is the challenge which Mr. Leighton offers. It is an acceptance of an educative concept of Youth Service able to stand in its own right, but which can also be accepted and practised by the Churches.

But within that Service, and because of that Service, the Church may properly seek to engage in a process of instruction for those seen to be responding to the Christian way of life. The Christian can no longer expect its own leaders and workers to do this as part of the Youth Service. It is a responsibility which the Church, as the Church – and not merely as a partner with the state – alone can accept.

Mr. Leighton's terms of reference are related to the first of these functions of participation in work among young people. They need to be accepted and applied to all Church Youth Work as an important contribution of the Church's service to the community and a genuine desire to meet young people's needs. The second function, Christian instruction and evangelism (a word I am not ashamed to use), needs as much careful thought and preparation as the first. Without the first, the Church may have little or no opportunity to do the second. But given both, the Church may well express in twentieth century terms, what Jesus himself did when he also was involved in a Teaching ministry.

Chapter One

The Development of a Youth Service

Whilst a clear date can be given to the inception of the *Service of Youth* through the Board of Education Circular 1486 to all local education authorities, the early beginnings of youth work and the reasons for them are less clear and not so easily chronclied. We can say, however, that the foundations of modern youth work were set somewhere in the second half of the 19th century although the reasons or need for such movements which came into being in that period were rooted in events which had changed dramatically the structure of British society during the previous century. This change was brought about by the move from an agrarian society to an urbanized one, and the effect this had on the main 'socialization' agencies, namely the family, the church and the immediate community. The family has always been thought of as the institution most strongly shaping, or socializing, the young in the way it passes on standards, values, opinions, taboos, rights and wrongs. For many centuries prior to the onset of the Industrial Revolution in the second half of the 18th century the family, whether in close proximity to numbers of other families or in comparative isolation, was likely to be a closely knit unit extending beyond two generations and through marriage. Economically it depended on all, including the children, for labour and production in order that it might survive. Whilst there would be a division of labour within the family group there was no division of time into working hours and non-working hours as we know it today. This is not to say that there was no time when people of the pre-industrial era relaxed from their labours, but the rosy picture of a tranquil and idyllic rural Britain is probably a false one, certainly for the masses of working people. The fairs, markets and feast-day celebrations would be an opportunity for people from a wider area than the hamlet or village to meet together and engage in some sport but again many of these special days would be allied to trading or bartering.

In such a society, close-knit, restricted in movement, lacking the means of communication which we now take for granted, the way of life would be simple and passed on from one generation to the next almost unchallenged. The order of things with 'the poor man at his gate and the rich man in his castle' – a line from a well-known and oft sung hymn, would be accepted as God's plan. The Church, very central in the lives of the people, and the State as personified in the Lord of the Manor or Squire would support and help to maintain this sort of society. For young people life would be ordered and the major influences affecting their development would subscribe to the same morality, to an acceptable code of behaviour. In this sense conflict would be generally absent, for the simple 'rightness' or 'wrongness' of thought or deed would be well known to everyone and one behaved 'rightly' within the prescribed code. Any behaviour outside the code would be sinful and punishable. There was little room for the individual who may have wished to challenge the system for it was hardly conceivable that the common man had the right to play such a role. But for the majority the well-ordered, simple, God-fearing and 'know your place' type of society meant security, for it was seen as man's destiny, and it may have been easier for young people to grow-up in a climate where rights and wrongs were so absolute. This is not to say that we desire this for man today but 'we shall go wrong if we look for this same type of social conscience as we are accustomed to now'.[1]

A convenient date to mark the beginning of the Industrial Revolution or Evolution is 1760, but obviously it was not so sudden or precise. The development of new sources of power and invention of machines in the cotton industry, the discovery of new processes in smelting coupled with the widening world's markets and a need for greater productivity led to the movement of people to the centres of industry and the beginning of organization and the growth of new towns. This gave rise to a new class structure of owners and workers; fixed hours of work and thus leisure-time or non-working time; change in the economy; rises in the cost of living; badly planned towns and cities; change in the function and influence of the family; employment of

[1] *Youth will be Led* – Alicia C. Percival: Collins. (Chapter 1)

women and children in factories and mines. In time these conditions produced social unrest, riots and unemployment. The ills of such changes rested very heavily on the young for the main agencies affecting their development were going through a difficult period of adjustment to the new way of life. 'Industrialism, in some respects rapidly and radically, in others more gradually, and imperceptibly, had altered the face of the country and profoundly modified the nature of society. Many of the institutions, for example, which previously had protected and controlled the young disappeared or acquired vastly different functions. The family, though not necessarily "weaker", was much affected by the demand that many more fathers *and* mothers go *out* to work and obey the rigid discipline of the factory bell'.[1]

By the middle of the 19th century we had a new industrial-urban society contrasting sharply with the previous predominantly rural society of the previous century.

Action was taken in three major areas affecting children and young people. First, in employment to regulate hours of work, the age at which children were employable and the conditions in which they worked; second, in education through the Sunday school movement, the establishment of nursery schools and, by 1876, making school attendance compulsory although it was not until 1899 that the leaving age was raised to twelve; third, in the use of leisure time, through clubs and 'organizations'. We should also recognize that this period produced, through the writings of Freud, Jung and Adler, new thoughts and concepts about the causes of man's behaviour. There was the beginnings of recognition of the period between childhood and manhood or womanhood as having significant factors in the development of a person. The theories of the early psychologists, challenging the moral philosophy of the day, and calling for deeper perceptions and more scientific analysis of the causes of man's behaviour were ridiculed and discredited. It is unlikely that they had much effect at the time on those individuals and agencies desiring greater protection of the young. In fact it is only comparatively recently that developmental psychology has taken its place alongside the respectable academic studies.

[1] *The Social Education of the Adolescent*–Davies and Gibson, U.L.P. 1967.

The concern was centred around the young worker, those affected directly by the conditions prevailing in the new organizations of the country. The selected young people who were fortunate enough to have the advantages of higher education were not included in such a concern for they were seen to be in less moral danger, and in fact would be so. Undoubtedly the 'Anti-social' problem children, the poor living and working conditions in the industrial areas, the movement of young people away from their homes to take up apprenticeship in commerce and industry, the exploitation of young labour and the changing influence of the home and church aroused in individuals and groups of adults the urge to work on behalf of the 'underprivileged'. Action took many forms, most of it individualistic and localized, attempting to meet immediate problems and according to whatever values the individual believed desirable for all men. It may have been by teaching the young to read, often the Bible in the belief that to get back to the daily reading of the 'good book' would alter man's condition; through evening classes for young domestics; recreational hours for young factory workers; organized games for 'working lads', camping and a study of nature and so on. Two points emerge from this:

1. *The growth of voluntary and philanthropic agencies.* Although government was taking some direct action to protect the young through the Factory, Apprenticeship and Education Acts, there was, and still is, resistance to direct action in the area of man's existence which falls loosely into the category of social or private life. This resistance in the last century may have been strongest in those who were in more favourable situations, but it was from the 'privileged' rather than the working class that the pioneers in all forms of social reform came. Help was given, as said earlier, around a localized problem and came in many forms through time, talents and money, to improve the lot of people. There was little, if any, structured approach to youth work, even in the way we know it today. '. . . in its early stages all this work was in the hands not so much of the voluntary organizations as of volunteers, individual men and women who pioneered with small groups of young people in neighbourhoods where overcrowding and disorderly behaviour, poverty and

drunkenness most attracted their reforming zeal. Before they began this work, almost the only non-commercialized provision for the leisure time of the poor was made by the Sunday Schools and the Salvation Army.'[1]

From some of these pioneer approaches movements evolved, such as the Y.M.C.A., Y.W.C.A., Boys' Brigade, Scouts, and from these, or parallel to them, others like the Girls' Brigade, Life Boys' Brigade, Church Lads' Brigade and the Boys' Clubs and Girls' Clubs movements as we know them today have their roots in individual clubs started at this time. But it is difficult to assess how much work was done by individuals in that period, or to know what were their aims and purposes, lost to us because it was not recorded. Because so many efforts were financed by the pioneers themselves or by benefactors disposed to help a cause they would be at the mercy of such philanthropy and undoubtedly many ceased to function because the source of financial backing dried-up, or because benefactors lost interest or could not see a return for their outlay. It would also be likely that the sponsors would want to direct the way in which the group functioned – a situation not unknown to us today!

2. *The leaders and 'the led'*. Towards the end of the 19th century a pattern of leadership was evolving. It was, perhaps, unquestionable and impractical that leadership could be invested in any but those who came from the privileged classes (although it is doutbful if George Williams of the Y.M.C.A. thought of himself as privileged). In their turn they would see leadership as their duty, not always as a right, and in a society which had moved quickly in historical terms from a feudal-type system to an urbanized situation the 'common man' would still look to the upper class for such forms of leadership in his social as well as his working life. This is no argument that it should always be so – or can be so. In fact during this period the working classes were demonstrating a capacity to organize and produce leadership in spheres which touched on their working lives, through co-operative movements, working men's clubs, insurance schemes and other 'protective' enterprises. To some of the industrial masters this must have seemed a great threat and

[1] *Youth and Youth Groups* – J. Macalister Brew: Faber and Faber 1957.

'many of them clearly viewed both working class self-help and even, ironically, the commerical enterprise which had helped to make them rich, as potentially dangerous to their own class if given encouragement in the field of social education'.[1] So for one reason or another, fear of the outcome of the working man being more involved in decision-making for himself in all the areas of his life, which might challenge those lessons which had been passed on by one class of people to another unquestioned in a different sort of society; or simply a belief that the common man was incapable of possessing those attributes of leadership because he lacked 'background, breeding and education', there would be resistance, at least no encouragement, to movements independent of adult leadership and such leadership coming from a particular class. 'But these early pioneers, the great ones . . . set a pattern of work which is still the blue print of most youth work, and more is owed to them than is ever acknowledged. The inspiration of leadership and love of humanity of one man or woman who gathered a band of friends together and proceeded to attract young people into an aura of friendship and worthwhile pursuits were of the essence of youth work from the beginning . . . It is true that much of the work was often tinged with patronage and flavoured with a kind of piety which is distasteful today, but that it made an incalcuable contribution to the lives of many young people in an age when few cared for them is indisputable and should not be lightly dismissed.'[2] We can question words like 'inspiration' in the light of a more scientific definition of the role of the youth worker and the purpose of youth work today, and 'worthwhile pursuits' in terms of what or by whose criteria a pursuit becomes worthwhile, but we should recognize, through all the patronage and piety, a caring for individuals or, more likely, numbers of young people in the same distress situations, and a love of humanity springing from religious feelings. That leadership was often more intuitive than scientific, a demonstration of what they believed to be their duty or calling, and in the main dealing with 'survival' needs, is undoubtedly true. The effects of the industrializing and urbanizing of much of the country in

[1] *The Social Education of the Adolescent*; ibid.
[2] *Youth and Youth Groups*; ibid.

terms of man's needs was not to be fully understood for another century and we have reason to suggest that it is not fully understood today. Could the early pioneers have acted differently in their society? Were the recipients overconcerned about patronage and piety when their immediate needs were being met?

No historical account, no matter how brief, can omit to mention the development of boys' and girls' clubs, the growth of uniformed organizations and the work of the University settlements of the second half of the last century. Generally they were single sexed with a strong religious connection. Few, if any of the pioneers, saw themselves starting something which would become a national movement – much less an international one. Ideas put into practice in one unit or club were picked up by others almost by chance, and some ideas for activity were so appealing that they in turn became the basis for a new youth movement. Scouting is an obvious example of an idea for the occupation of boys becoming part of another movement (the Boys' Brigade) and also resulting in a youth movement through the spontaneous formation of groups of young people who found the idea of Baden-Powell's 'Scouting for Boys' appealing. It seems a pity that the response by girls to this activity resulted in a separate movement (Girl Guides) for it could well have been the first 'national' mixed youth organization![1]

By the turn of the century there was a new 'intellectual' climate and a decline in the Evangelical influence. There was a new determination to eradicate poverty and deal with the poor housing conditions of the majority of the population. Minimum standards of space and sanitation were being enforced and local authorities were empowered to clear slum areas and build houses. Some enlightened employers had built houses and created their own towns and 'model villages' (Bournville and Port Sunlight). In 1898 Ebenezer Howard proposed that the whole freehold of 'garden cities' must be kept in public ownership for the sake of planning control. This attention to the poor living conditions of so many people influenced the spread of clubs for young people and the growth of 'settlements'. The increase in evening provision through 'night-schools' attended

[1] For a chronological time-table of the founding of youth movements see Appendix A.

by many young people pursuing some form of further education, mostly vocational, prior to 1918, reflected not only the desire on the part of the working class young person to continue his learning in the hope of better prospects but also to satisfy some of his social and leisure time needs. Many 'night schools' offered opportunities for recreation within the time-table and supported extra-curricula games and pastimes.

The First World War (1914–1918) effected the development of youth work in a number of ways. The total population was involved in the war effort and again young people were to suffer most through the change in the influence of the home. With fathers away and mothers working in factories the young 'cut loose' with a resultant rise in juvenile delinquency. The Home Office and the Board of Education combined to draw the attention of the government and local authorities to this problem and to propose certain ways of remedying the unhealthy situation. A central body known as the Juvenile Organizations Committee was formed in 1916 with the brief '. . . to make suggestions to combat the rising incidence of delinquency, to help and encourage voluntary organizations to see that leisure time occupations and facilities were provided for young people and to give a general eye to their social welfare'. Local authorities were asked to establish local J.O.C.'s obviously with the same brief. This concern with delinquency, coupling it with leisure time 'occupations' through youth organizations, still with us, created a climate of opinion which associates youth work with particular groups of young people, and sees the task as a remedial one. The increase in taxation meant a decrease in the 'voluntary' financial contributors to youth movements and the inevitable governmental and the local authorities financial cuts after the war reducing what little aid had been made possible during the war years only served to show a lack of concern for young people except in times of emergency or crisis. By inaugurating J.O.C.'s the 'state' had intervened in something which had been, up to now, a voluntary movement. Youth work was set to follow the pattern of so much of the social service provision, namely individual action relying on voluntaryism and philanthropy, then state intervention and some aid but still maintaining the voluntary nature of the provision, then the state 'filling in the gaps' and inaugurating provision but still permitting some voluntary provision and finally taking over the total task of provision. Not all services or provision including youth work have reached this final stage of total provision by the state.

Between the First and Second World Wars the country faced a bleak period of industrial unrest leading to strikes, an economic depression resulting in 20 per cent of the working population being unemployed, a change in Britain's world position, the fear of war coming from an uneasy Europe, and naturally a lowering of morale and loss of faith in self, organization and government. At a time when so many young people were leaving school only to join the queue at the Unemployment Exchange ('the dole') with no signs of a job in the near, or any, future; when it was difficult for many to remember the last hot meal and time was all one had, youth clubs and organizations were some little compensation.[1] They were kept in being by grants from large trusts or by the efforts of local businessmen. Some local authorities exercised the permissive power through the Fisher Act of 1918, to make available funds and premises and encourage teachers to establish Old Scholars' Clubs, but generally the picture was a dismal one.

In 1936 the British Medical Association's Report alarmed the country with comments on the poor physical state of health of the youth of Britain. In comparison reports from the Continent spoke highly of the physical health of the young in Czechoslavakia and Germany and the strength of the respective youth movements, Sokol and Hitler Jugend. The B.M.A. report made greater impact than the Report on the need for Youth Community Centres on New Housing Estates published in 1936 by the Board of Education Juvenile Organizations Committee. The Board of Education and the Ministry of Health had 'no hesitation in commending this Report to the sympathetic considerations of Local Authorities.' The Report noted that about a quarter of the population of England and Wales were now living in new houses on new estates at or near existing towns and, further, that juvenile organizations and everyone else concerned in working among young persons were held up on these new estates by the lack of facilities. Still the emphasis was on voluntary effort and local authorities were asked to give 'sympathetic

[1] *Disinherited Youth*: A Survey 1936–1939. Carnegie United Kingdom Trust 1943.

considerations' to a situation brought about by continued urbanization, estates planned with little or no social amenities particularly for youth, nor for adults in so many cases, and yet the Report showed that 'more than half of the population of new housing estates is under the age of 18'.

The outbreak of war in 1939 forced the government to action on behalf of young people above school leaving age and the Board of Education, in its circular 1486 entitled *Service of Youth*, said it had decided to undertake a direct responsibility for youth welfare and urged local education authorities for Higher Education to co-operate with voluntary bodies in the provision for the social and physical development of boys and girls, which it said, had long been neglected in this country. Obviously what had happened to young people during the 1914–1918 war had quite an influence on the committee appointed by the Board of Education in October 1939 to advise on problems of juvenile welfare in war-time. The main points of the circulars were:

1. A determination to prevent the physical, moral and mental deterioration of young people during war-time. The strain of war and disorganization of family life, together with the black-out, emphasized the defects in our social services;
2. A National Youth Committee appointed to advise the President of the Board of Education and to provide central guidance and leadership to the movement throughout the country;
3. The re-opening of clubs and a request for the release of premises requisitioned for war purposes: a recommendation for financial assistance, through voluntary organizations, to help clubs hire premises, secure leaders and instructors;
4. A call to local education authorities and voluntary bodies to work together in free and equal partnership: the establishment of local Youth Committees and the appointment of a Secretary: local education authorities to inform the President of the Board of arrangements for constituting Youth Committees by 1st March, 1940;
5. The young people themselves must be encouraged to find new constructive outlets for their leisure time and for voluntary national service.

There were a number of fears and suspicions aroused by the circular, notably the fear of a National Youth Movement similar to those on the continent of Europe and the arranged marriage between the voluntary bodies and the local education authorities. This was seen as a shotgun marriage rather than a desirable partnership. Voluntary financial help was drying up, manpower was at a premium and the voluntary unit was probably less able to get round restrictions than the local authority. It also appeared that the local authorities were being seen as the senior partners.

By March 1940, 111 of the 146 authorities had informed the Board of some action and 65 had schemes for local youth committees. In June of that year the Board issued circular 1516 *The Challenge of Youth* which was 'to give some guidance on the general aim and purpose of the work'. In saying that 'the general aim was to be found in the social and physical training, which links all youth organizations to one another and to the schools' the Youth Service was placed firmly in the educational service. The circular allayed the early fears of a national youth movement for 'any attempt of a state-controlled uniformity or regimentation would be both stupid and perilous: more than that, it would be wholly alien to the spirit of the country'. It also reminded the partners that there need be no clash between them for 'the field is so large and the range so wide that there is ample room for a vast extension of effort'. There was a mild rebuke, too, in the statement about 'the goodwill which may be expected to exist among all concerned with work for youth'.

The uniformed youth organizations at this time recruited large numbers to their units, many young people viewing this as an apprenticeship to the parent body they hoped to join at the appropriate age. The purpose of such organizations was clear, that of the non-uniformed clubs less clear because it was not so easily identifiable with the war-effort. In 1942 all young people between 16 and 18 were requested to register by order under powers taken by Defence Regulations. The purpose was to encourage those who had not linked up with the voluntary youth organizations, to do so and 'share with their fellows in a common endeavour'. What the procedure brought to light could not have been envisaged by those who sought the powers to register these young people. Interviewers discovered that young people were working extremely long hours, many in unsatisfactory conditions with long travel to and from work and little leisure time. A year later the government proposed a review of working hours of this age group, proposing 48 hours per week, the possibility of transfer to work nearer home, supplementary feeding and a need for those concerned with young people in industry and organizations to see that they had adequate rest. Canteens – very much a term of the time – became a most important and central part of the programme, with a very generous points allowance for food which was heavily rationed to the normal household, and a desire that young people should not be heavily programmed to the extent that relaxing or 'doing nothing' became respectable!

The Education Act of 1944, the result of much controversy about the content of education, placed the youth service within further education and called for its extension. The notion of the County College[1] would have given all young people over school leaving age and up to the age eighteen compulsory day release with the possibility of pursuing vocational studies and joining non-vocational groups through some form of student union or council. Perhaps it is unfortunate that such a notion was not to be a practicality, although many youth workers saw such a development as a threat to their units of work and the arguments they used then were used again about the Newsom concept and are still used today about the development of youth work within the secondary school. This is all the more strange when the youth service can lay some claims to having pioneered working with young people in this informal way for their total development.

Immediate Post-War Years 1945–1950

During the war years young people's worth had been recognized mostly in terms of the parts they had played in the fighting areas where they had experienced a new kind of independence. They had been forced to take adult roles at an earlier stage in their development than would have been possible without a war. The adolescent period was reduced by expediency. This, and the uncertainty about life, meant that they were indulged in so many ways which would have brought sharp rebuke a decade before. Horizons had been extended by war-time experiences

[1] See Education Act 1944 Sections – 41 and 53.

and they were unlikely to want to take up life as it was before and although the years in uniform may not have been desired they would not be wasted or lost years as they were to so many older people. So many young people were still in the forces and still being conscripted in the immediate post-war years that the country was not to feel the full impact of their reactions till the mid-fifties. Having witnessed young people both at the battle front and on the home front exercising a high degree of responsibility, imagination, enterprise and fortitude when the challenge was clear it was surprising that we did not know how to offer similar challenges to young people after the war. Very soon we slipped back to thinking of young people, if not now as juveniles, certainly as needing chaperonage in the youth service. Leadership was to be from some special sort of person and standards of leadership were based on personality qualities and amount of experience. Take this quotation from the report of the Committee on Recruitment, Training and Conditions of Service of Youth Leaders and Community Centre Wardens (1949): 'We found it necessary to consider first the qualities that are to be looked for in candidates who are to be recruited and trained for work with young people. If the standards of the Youth Service are to be maintained and improved its leaders must be men and women who can bring to bear on the young people they are working with influences which may be broadly described as educational. The most important qualifications needed are a sound educational background, broad interests, and alert and cultivated minds, a quick and sympathetic understanding of young people, stability and maturity of outlook, and the power to stimulate and direct interests and activities. The work demands considerable physical stamina and vitality.' No mention in this, or other parts of this report, that young people had been asked what they looked for in a leader – adult or not – or that the committee had thought of leadership from the point of view of young people. The report also distinguishes between social and educational in a way which reflected the debate that was a common feature of training weekends, conferences and meetings at that time, viz, is youth work social or educational? Furthermore, accepting that the Report was concerned with training for full-time work, it emphasized time after time that working with young people was an exhausting job and only for the 23–35 age group. The teachers at that time could not have taken kindly to the suggestion that after that age one should move from the 'exhausting' youth service to the less exhausting school or class-room.

The sort of phrases, culled from government and other reports, like 'building of character', 'developing the whole personality' and 'moral, mental and physical development' became the easily stated purposes of youth work at that time. It bred the balanced programme approach to club work which tended to produce blue prints for nightly meetings with something physical, something intellectual and finalizing it all with an epilogue or short prayers. Production, in far too many cases, was the yardstick of success and membership was evaluated in terms of participation in a preconceived programme. Whilst some organizations, authorities and single units were encouraging greater participation by the young in some form of democratic self-government and self-programming the general picture was of young people playing a game of being democratic inside a fairly autocratic structure.

The Lean Years 1950–1958

Public opinion was not strong enough on the side of the Youth Service to warrant any special pronouncement or provision in the ten years after the war. On the one hand there was a feeling that young people had never had it so good, that far too much was done for them, and on the other that they were creating no problems. This was to change in the middle fifties. Local education authorities faced a 5 per cent cut in expenditure in 1951 and these two factors alone meant little advancement in the service at national and local level. If youth work was seen either as remedial or a 'frill' it would naturally suffer from lack of funds and poor public opinion. In many parts of the country voluntary help had been hard to come by, perhaps a repercussion from compulsory war service, and there had been an increase in paid part-time help, either as leaders or instructors. Now the authorities had to look carefully at their expenditure and it became more difficult to meet all the requirements of paid staff, grants for equipment and maintenance. In 1952 there was a reduction in expenditure on buildings which resulted almost in a stop to building new centres. The recruitment to full-time training was falling far short of the places available and the training agencies, notably the Universities, ceased to offer courses. This was undoubtedly due to the uncertainty of a career in the youth service in such a precarious situation.

Young people were beginning to make themselves felt in the mid-fifties and when Bill Haley's 'Rock Around the Clock' hit town with the most unpredicable reaction at the Elephant and Castle the scene was set for a kind of teenage revolution. Suddenly we realized that there were a lot of them and more than there had ever been before in our history, and that they were intent on letting us know exactly how they felt. It would be completely wrong to see this 'revolution' only in terms of violent or person to person violent terms. The desire to break away from tradition and formality, which was seen as 'square', to more free and expressive terms was manifest in their music, art, dance forms, dress, hair styles and what they supported or protested about. They reflected, much too sharply for many adults, the rejection of authority and the challenge to the Establishment by much of society and they were intent on deciding for themselves about issues which in previous generations young people had 'accepted', with little challenge, from their elders. This caused some estrangement between the ages. It also caused rifts within the teenage peer group.

Since 1939, with state intervention, the Youth Service had developed more by accident than national design except for the war years when the emphasis was on the prevention of moral decline of the young and service to the nation. The biggest single development, as much due to lack of resources as to the fact that men and women were operating on more equal terms during the war than had been the case hitherto, was in the growth of mixed clubs. This was where the local education authorities began to be seen as club-sponsoring bodies. An important part of their function was to 'fill in the gaps' left by the national organizations and they were more likely to see a boys' and girls' club as the need rather than two separate units serving the same area. It was also in line with the development of co-education in schools. The National Association of Girls' Clubs, having become the National Association of Girls' Clubs and Mixed Clubs changed to Mixed and Girls' Clubs and more latterly, to the National Association of Youth Clubs. Boys' Clubs have remained so and the National Association of Boys' Clubs formed in 1924 still makes out a case for a boys-only type of organization although many Boys' Clubs invite girls into their organization for special programmes. Both these associations are affiliating bodies, that is, they will consider for membership clubs which meet their minimum requirements.

The Methodist Association of Youth Clubs, formed in 1945, reflected the Church's approach to youth work in the post-war period. The Church saw the dual need of serving its members, that is, young people who had taken or who were desirous of taking Church membership and other young people of the area served by the local Church. This sort of approach was to be termed 'open' club work, being different to 'closed clubs' serving only those who belonged to the Church.[1]

As one should expect the uniformed organizations lost members and to a certain degree were unable to define a purpose as clear as that of the 1939–1945 period in order to attract young people. Uniforms were not so popular after the war! The paramilitary type organizations suffered the most but the others like Scouts, Guides and Brigades also lost members, particularly in the upper age bracket. To many they are seen as juvenile organizations – this could be said of many clubs, too, but the tendency is to think of the latter as youth or young adult organizations. Another development in the club-type approach was the single purpose group. This was a complete reversal, it seemed, of the argument for a balanced programme of a few years earlier. Canoe, drama, climbing, music, athletics, motor cycle and similar interest, or hobby groups, became respectable and 'recognizable' by authorities. The single-purpose organization, the Young Farmers' Association had been in existence since 1920 and recognized by the Youth Service and perhaps in time the political youth groups will be recognized as a part of a comprehensive youth service. Young people were becoming vocal about youth clubs and organizations and those responsible for the youth service were beginning to see the need for work

[1] For a fuller account of the development of Youth work in the Methodist Church see *The Emancipation of Youth* by Douglas S. Hubery.

with spontaneous groups or gangs. Correspondence in *The Times* in 1952 following a leading article on the publication of *The Young Wage Earner* (a review of young people in Glasgow) referred to such groups as 'unattached' – a term which has remained with us and is too often used in a derogatory sense.

To talk of a pattern in the Youth Service in the middle fifties would be misleading. There was certainly a 'sameness' about youth clubs and organizations throughout the country and whilst this would be expected in the units of the uniformed organizations clubs had shown little enterprise in experiment or in being different in the general approach to serving the needs of young people. Resources through the local authorities and sponsors were limited but little attempt was made to involve the community in paying for the service. The general public could hardly be blamed for this for they had no clear understanding of what the Youth Service was and could only express their thoughts in negative terms like 'it keeps them off streets' and 'it finds them something to do'. Since the war there had been no national pronouncement about the youth service and those responsible at local level had not seen the value of a public relations job aimed at soliciting support or considered it none of the public concern. Perhaps they had little faith in what they were doing. This would not be so in all parts of the country for there were those local authorities and national organizations who, despite the financial burden and lack of esteem for the service, were developing by appointing more field staff, training voluntary workers and senior members, organizing youth rallies and festivals of various kinds, opening outdoor pursuits centres, encouraging holidays abroad and displaying to the public the work done by clubs and organizations.

Within each local authority area patterns began to emerge. Some local authorities developed their own Youth Service with scant attention to the work done in their area by the national voluntary organizations, others saw their function as serving the voluntary organizations and not taking any initiative in forming new groups and some made efforts to work in close partnership with all the bodies concerned with youth. By now we were accustomed to the terms L.E.A. clubs and voluntary organizations, not always used in a complimentary sense but rather in terms of merit.

If there was little public outcry for more effort to be made the Standing Conference of National Voluntary Youth Organizations, King George's Jubilee Trust and the National Association of (Local Education Authorities) Youth Officers were voicing great concern about the state of the Youth Service. Their pleas were reinforced in 1957 by the Report from the Select Committee on Estimates appointed by the government 'to examine such of the Estimates presented to this House as may seem fit to the Committee, and to report what, if any, economies consistent with the policy implied in those Estimates may be effected therein . . . '. The Committee chose to look at the Estimates relating to the Youth Employment Service and the Youth Service Grants, and in respect of the latter took evidence from representatives of King George's Jubilee Trust, S.C.N.V.Y.O. and the Association of Education Committees. There was criticism of both the amount of money spent by the Ministry of Education in grants to national organizations and how this was apportioned. What came out of the committee's Report was not proposed economies but 'the impression . . . that the Ministry is little interested in the present state of the Service and apathetic about its future. Your Committee considers that this apathy is having a deeply discouraging effect on the valuable work done for the Service, much of it voluntary and unpaid, and must thereby be reacting unfavourably on the value for money obtained from the Grants'. And further '. . . the Ministry . . . should ensure that they are properly discharging their duty in respect of the Youth Service, that they should formulate a policy and state it publicly, and that they should not let the service drift into a state where the present grants will be wasted'.

Such expressions in a government report strengthened the argument of those in the Youth Service and provided an opportunity for those members of both Houses of Parliament who were well disposed to youth work to challenge the Minister. In November 1958 the Minister appointed a Committee, under the chairmanship of the Countess of Albemarle 'to review the contribution which the youth service of England and Wales can make in assisting young people to play their part in the life of the community, in the light of changing social and industrial conditions and of current trends in other branches of the education service: and to advise according to what priorities best value can be obtained for the money spent'. The Committee presented its report[1] some twelve months later and it was presented to Parliament in February 1960. Whatever the feelings of those in the Service at the time of the enquiry – and there was widespread suspicion that the Committee would give the Minister grounds for 'killing off' the Service – the Report did nothing but justify the need for such a Service for youth and proposed advancements on all fronts.

A Ten Year Development Plan

The first five years of the development plan were seen as 'catching up with the situation already upon us.' The Youth Service was seen as facing two emergencies. One was the increase in the number of young people and the ending of national service and the other the concern about young people who were demonstrating withdrawal from society. The local education authorities had been empowered through the 1944 Education Act to provide a varied and comprehensive educational service in their areas and the wording gave such wide powers that almost any reasonable provision for groups of people was possible. Evidence to the committee, however, suggested that these powers were not being exercised 'in accordance with the spirit and intention of Parliament'. An effective lead was needed and the Committee believed that this should come from the Minister and 'that he should foster efforts (of youth workers) by more positive and consistent guidance . . .' The second five years was envisaged as consolidating by securely establishing a permanent structure. In this respect the Committee proposed the setting up of a Youth Service Development Council to advise the Minister on matters related to the ten year plan. Members of this Council to be appointed not on a representative basis but 'men and women who have special qualities and experience to offer'.

Aims and Ideals

To justify the need for a Youth Service the Committee argued the case for not ending abruptly the social and intellectual development of those young persons not going on to the other forms of full-time education after their secondary education. It

[1] *The Youth Service in England and Wales* H.M.S.O. 1960.

contrasted the leisure available to those who left formal education at 15 with that provided by the state for those more fortunate and compared 'the standard of premises usual in organizations within the Youth Service with those of a residential hostel or undergraduates common room in almost any redbrick university'. The Report quoted Sir John Maud's[1] statement of the aims of a Youth Service.

'To offer individual young people in their leisure time opportunities of various kinds, complementary to those of home, formal education and work, to discover and develop their personal resources of body, mind and spirit and thus the better equip themselves to live the life of mature, creative and responsible members of a free society.' But went on to say, 'The aim of the Youth Service is not to remove tensions so as to reach towards some hypothetical condition of "adjustment" to individual or social life. It is to help towards ensuring that those tensions which are social accidents, often both fruitless and oppressive, shall not submerge the better possibilities of children during their adolescence.'

This was speaking more to the needs of young people in relation to the contemporary scene than the Maud statement and the committee was realistic in its comments that not all young people would wish to belong to the Youth Service, seeing many of them going it alone or remaining 'unattached'. At the same time it did not make it clear that a Youth Service could be seen as offering opportunities to individual young people to take whatever they wanted from it to suit their purpose without committing themselves to the Service. This *could* be read into Maud's statement.

The Albemarle Report offered a new triology of association, training and challenge. It saw association as meeting the need for young people from different backgrounds to maintain and develop their sense of fellowship, of mutual respect and tolerance. Centres offering such an opportunity may also 'help to counteract the increasing educational and professional stratification of society'. To this was added the need for young people to be helped to make sound judgements, to differentiate between 'the

[1] *Youth Service Tomorrow*: a report of a meeting arranged by King George's Jubilee Trust 1951.

excitements offered in each day's passing show' and those things 'slower and more hardly won . . . more rewarding', which could suggest a value judgement, by adults' standards, of what is worthwhile in activity or perhaps it was the fear of what the Report was saying being interpreted as fun. It was rumoured that when the Report was before a particular local education committee an elected representative of the people said that – 'this is fun and we're not paying for fun'. There was still a need to justify programme content in narrow educational terms. The experiences of being together, of enjoyment and satisfaction in the short term are still questioned as to their worth in both formal and informal education. So to 'association of the *right kind* and training of *the right kind* (my italics) was added a third: challenge. This was seen in relation to new experiences both within the group and from outside to the group or individual and the way in which meeting challenge might enhance status and feeling of worth.

As with any such Report the reader takes from it what he wants and there were those in the Youth Service who saw the Report as doing nothing more than endorse what they were already doing, others saw it lacking in clear direction as to the way the Service should develop, some as a radical document, others saying the opportunity to be radical had been lost. Whatever line one took was not important, or less important than the fact that something had been said in some detail about youth, present society and Youth Service for the first time since the war with strong recommendations for action.

An Imaginative Building Programme

The Report called for a generous and imaginative building programme to rehabilitate the Youth Service and to equip for the expansion called for and asked the Minister to give attention to the design of premises for youth work. At local level, the Report said, the authorities and the voluntary organizations should work in partnership in planning and siting premises. Local educational authorities, it was proposed, should allow for the needs of the Youth Service in planning of new secondary schools.

Staffing and Training

The McNair Report[1] in 1942 estimated a need for five to six thousand full-time youth workers with a flow from training agencies of 300 per annum to meet replacements and wastage. At the end of the Second World War it was estimated there were about 6,000 full-time workers in England and Wales, but at the time of the Albemarle Report the number was 700. As with the McNair, Jackson and Fletcher reports the Albemarle Report did not see the Service becoming staffed entirely by full-time workers but made a case for the professional 'strategically placed'. The causes for the drift away from full-time work have been mentioned earlier. Now the Albemarle Report estimated, from evidence given by the local education authorities and voluntary organizations, a need for an increase to 1,300 full-time leaders by the end of the first years of the ten-year development plan and recommended both long-term training arrangements and an *emergency* training college offering a one-year course to 90 men and women in the first year and 140 in the succeeding years. This, together with those trained at Westhill Teachers' Training College, University of Swansea, University of Manchester, and by the N.A.B.C. and Y.M.C.A. to produce the required 1,300 by 1966. Subsequently it was seen that the estimated number was far short of requirements and developments and the *emergency* training course continued for a further four years. The Report indicated that full-time workers should be recruited from teaching and social work as well as 'mature persons with a natural gift for leadership' who would receive training at the *emergency* college or one of the training agencies mentioned above. The Minister was requested to set a date after which no new entrant to full-time leadership would be able to claim qualification by experience alone. As a number of such people were already being employed, local education authorities were asked to recommend to the Minister, for recognition as qualified, those full-time workers who had completed five years' service to the satisfaction of the authorities. Further, a committee to be appointed to negotiate scales of salaries and recommend conditions of employment. This was to be a tidying-up operation and a step towards professionalizing full-time work.

[1] *The Training of Teachers and Youth Workers*: H.M.S.O. 1942.

The McNair, Fletcher and Jackson Reports dealing with this question of recruitment, training and conditions of employment had not been implemented, but the Albemarle Report although recommending little difference in principle was implemented. The National College for the Training of Youth Leaders was opened in January 1961, nine months before the date suggested in the Report, and the Joint Negotiating Committee for Youth Leaders was appointed and issued its first report[1] in July 1961 setting out a salary scale and conditions of service.

Attention to full-time training may have overshadowed the remarkable development in part-time leadership training since 1960. The Bessey Report and the recommendation in the Albemarle Report that local education authorities and voluntary organizations should co-operate to organize schemes of part-time training were seized on with much enthusiasm and despite the fact that many original schemes followed slavishly the syllabus laid down in the Bessey Report, many who had worked in comparative isolation and newcomers to the Service obviously enjoyed and gained from the courses. One of the features of the Bessey type courses has been a reflection of the new approach to youth work which can be culled from the Albemarle Report. This is a desire by people working with young people in uniformed and structured organizations, in clubs, on the streets, in schools and social work to pursue a common course devoted to understanding the young person, to learn how to offer help to individuals, to gain some insights into group behaviour with a lessening concern for structures and prescriptions.

Implementation

Unlike many previous reports on the Youth Service the Albemarle Report was well received and the lead, so often requested in the last decade, was given by the Minister of Education. There was a new impetus and a reassurance of the worth of youth work. The Report had shown disparities in the service offered by local education authorities in terms of expenditure per head of the youth population: assistance to individual youth

[1] *First Report of the Negotiating Committee for Youth Leaders* – July 1961 (and subsequent reports).

groups; the employment of full-time staff and expenditure.[1] The estimated number of those young people belonging to clubs and organizations was 30 per cent of the total youth population. This was probably a generous estimate, not allowing for dual membership, but ignoring the many young people who had 'tried' the Service and either found it wanting or decided, quite healthily, that it did not meet their needs. However, there was a challenge to those in the field now that a lead and material help was offered to expand the Service and through this to 'attract more . . . young people'.

The 1960s saw changes in a number of directions, some of them not easily assessible at this time. Certainly there was much more thought given to shaping a service to meet the needs of young people in varying social situations and to involve them in the planning and running of their organizations. Self-programming by young people became a popular expression but how far this was firmly believed or allowed to operate is questionable. Limits are still set on the scope given to young people in managing their own service and adults in the service remain protective.[2] The term *Youth Leader* had been a matter for debate for many years. Leader smacked too much of an ideal type, of a person who always knows the way the 'followers' should go, who not only shows the way but takes people along his way and no matter how this was expressed 'by being in front "leading from behind" or, a nice compromise, "from within"', it was still seen as directive by someone who knows what is right for others. The term youth *worker* began to replace youth leader and all that this did at the time was to reflect dissatisfactions with the title and a desire to break down some of the barriers between the young and the adult. Attitudes and functions were not going to change as easily as changing titles. However, there was movement and the pendulum swung from directiveness in leadership to permissiveness – a peculiar sort of permissiveness which suggested that the leader, worker or adult in charge should have no influence on the lives of young people and that self-programming and self-determination meant the young could do

[1] See Appendix 4 of the Report *The Youth Service in England and Wales.*

[2] *Lady Albemarle's Boys* – Ray Gosling.

as they liked with no check or 'interference' by the adult worker. Perhaps this was inevitable and, like all pendulums, it swung from one extreme to another and it may be in the '70s we shall see it, not coming to rest, but swinging through a more central field.

Another important change in the sixties has been the shift of emphasis from *the* club or organization to the individual person. The service is now more client-centred than unit or organization centred and more will be said about this in Chapter Five.

Chapter Two

THE PRESENT STRUCTURE AND ORGANIZATION OF THE YOUTH AND COMMUNITY SERVICE

Responsibility for the youth service is shared by the Department of Education and Science, the local education authorities and the voluntary organizations which include the churches. This partnership exists throughout the education service in Britain with each partner having functions peculiar to it.

Department of Education and Science

The Board of Education circular 1516 in 1940 stated the function of the state is '. . . to focus and lead the efforts of all engaged in youth welfare; to supplement the resources of existing national organizations without impairing their independence; and to ensure through co-operation that the ground is covered in a way never so far attained'. From time to time, as we have seen, central government has expressed concern about youth welfare, usually in times of national crisis, and taken some lead in proposing ways to meet the needs. However, the central department was chiefly concerned with financial matters until the acceptance of the main recommendations of the Albemarle Report. This required a 'national policy' calling for direct action by the then Minister of Education.

Grants The Department of Education and Science gives direct grants to national voluntary youth organizations for the administration and organization of their headquarters and for training at national level. This list of bodies so aided has almost doubled since 1960 and includes the larger denominational youth organizations.

Building Programme In the period 1960 to 1968 the Department sanctioned £28 million worth of new building for the youth service. The money for these projects comes from the rating levies made by local authorities and the rate support grant from government funds. This is added to by local or national voluntary schemes.

Full-time Training To meet the emergency training suggested in the Albemarle Report the Department of Education and Science established a National College for the Training of Youth Leaders at Leicester. In such circumstances the central government meets the total finances incurred. When it feels that the emergency is over or that such training can be accommodated through the normal training schemes it withdraws its direct responsibility. The National College at Leicester came to an end in August 1970 and three new courses of two-year duration complemented those already in existence to provide the output of full-time community and youth workers, namely, College of Education of Leicester, Goldsmith's College in London and John Dalton College in Manchester.

Further to the National College the Department encouraged Colleges of Education to undertake a youth leadership option for teachers in training, available at about 50 such colleges at the moment.

Experimental Work Through the advice of the Youth Service Development Council the Department of Education and Science makes money available to national voluntary organizations or research organizations for experimental projects in approaches to work with young people. To gain such an award the organization has to show that it has the intention and facilities for documentation and the production of a final report on the project.

Part-time Training The Bessey Report of 1961 on the training of part-time workers, accepted by the Minister, recommended that the local education authorities and the voluntary organizations should set up joint training agencies. By 1963 some 110 of the 146 local education authorities in England and Wales reported that such bodies had been established.

The Youth Service Development Council This body may be seen as having similarities with the Juvenile Organizations Committee of 1916 and the National Youth Council of the 1930s but it has had the advantages of more direct action coming from its advice and recommendations to the Minister than the previous bodies. In 1967 one of its committees under the chairmanship of Lord Hunt presented the Report *Immigrants and the Youth Service*. This Committee's terms of reference were 'To consider the part which the Youth Service might play in meeting the needs of young immigrants in England and Wales and to make recommendations',[1] and the Secretary of State for Education and Science receiving the Report asked local education authorities and voluntary youth organizations to provide information about developments in furthering the integration of young 'coloured' immigrants.

In the recommendation of the Development Council the Secretary of State established, as a charitable trust, The Young Volunteer Force Foundation, which would employ young adults available to go to local areas, by invitation, to stimulate schemes of voluntary community service. The Foundation was to be an independent body depending on voluntary sources for income beyond the government grant which was £100,000 for the first year's work.

In March 1967 Mr. Denis Howell, Parliamentary Under-Secretary of State for Education and Science said, in the House of Commons 'One of the reasons that we are possibly failing in the Youth Service is that we are trying to do too much in one age band – 14 to 20. Young people at the top end of that age-range find very little identity with the people at the bottom end of that age-range. It therefore seems to me that both ends of the Youth Service age-range should be examined.' The Youth Service Development Council appointed two committees, one under the chairmanship of Mr. A. N. Fairbairn, Deputy Director of Education for the County of Leicestershire, to look at the relationship of the Youth Service with schools and further education; the other under the chairmanship of Dr. F. W. Milson, Senior Youth Tutor at Westhill College of Education, to study the relationship of the Youth Service with the adult community. The expectation 'in the field' was of two reports to be published. However after much delay *Youth and*

[1] *Immigrants and the Youth Service*: H.M.S.O. 1967.

Community Work in the 70's[1] was published in October 1969. The Reports of the two committees had been considerd by a working party of the Under-Secretary and the chairmen of the committees and this composite Report was produced. Delay in producing the Report; the very poor public relations work at its release (a number of newspapers made a meal out of the 'Chatting-up the birds' phrase from this unfortunate sentence in a main recommendation. 'A great many need help in developing their relations with the opposite sex: "Knowing how to chat up birds" was how one boy put it. *Therefore grant policy should favour mixed work*'); the fact that authorities were being asked to prune expenditure; the unimaginative and almost old fashioned view of the value of activities in Chapter XIII; a lack of clarity in the use of the term community work and a feeling by many part-time and full-time workers of unrealism in the pattern of work being proposed, were some of the reasons for its cool reception. In comparison with the Albemarle Report, *Youth and Community Work in the 70's* was to be seen as a document for debate at all levels of Youth work and Howell asked the authorities, voluntary organizations, professional associations and training agencies to submit their comments to him by the end of 1969. From these and the recommendations in the Report he would make an announcement about the future of the Youth Service early in 1970. The Statement was eventually made on 29th March, 1971, by the Secretary of State, Mrs. Margaret Thatcher, to the effect that 'the (Youth) Service in England and Wales should continue on its present basis, but with certain changes of emphasis, which should be reflected by corresponding changes in the financial support given by the Department (of Education and Science)', and further 'the Government do not think it would be right to change the nature of the Service in England and Wales radically by setting up a Youth and Community Service with not very clearly defined responsibilities'.

The main policy-making proposals in the Report are worth summarizing here, but the Report should be studied in full to assess the weight of argument for such proposals.

1. A Youth and Community Service should be established which will get away from the club-is-the-Youth Service

[1] *Youth and Community Work in the 70's*: H.M.S.O. 1969.

approach, meet the needs of young people by making contact with them *wherever* they are to be found, and recognize them as part of the community.

2. In a service designed to meet the needs of individuals it is neither necessary nor desirable to lay down hard and fast dividing lines: in practice we see the change of emphasis in youth work at about the age 16 or 17.

3. Work among the younger age groups should be mainly the responsibility of the schools and voluntary organizations, working either in unison or independently. The existing Youth Service lower age limit of 14 should disappear.

4. We hope the advance already made in developing youth work in schools and colleges will gather momentum. . . . We believe that joint appointments covering youth and education can be a major factor in breaking down barriers. We should like to see more of them.

5. The pattern of the Youth and Community Service for the upper age-range must be governed by a clear recognition of their adult status and level of sophistication. This may include, for example, the right of the over 18's to have alcoholic drinks in sponsored organizations . . . There should be no upper age limit since people will use the service as long as they need it.

6. We must shed the idea that the Youth and Community Service is primarily concerned with buildings, organizations or membership.

7. The new Youth and Community Service will bring exciting possibilities for new partnerships between the Service and industry, trade unions, commercial enterprises, and social services and education.

8. The acceptance of our view of youth and community work has clear implications for the training of Youth and Community workers. . . . We endorse the new training proposed for a two-year course (to replace the one year course) and feel this is a step in the right direction.

The term Service of Youth was now superseded by the term Youth and Community Work. This was in fashion with other developments in allied social work – the word 'community' was prefixing so many titles or definitions of working with people. Community work was the 'in-thing' and this is not said in any way to disparage community work, but the term was being used far too loosely as though using it gave more meaning or value to the original work. It is interesting to note in some instances, notably in training, the transposition of the words so that we had Community and Youth Work implying that community is a study and youth work the task or function of the trainees. There was sufficient evidence that youth work was getting away from the club-is-the-youth service as the only approach but there was ample evidence that some young people, a substantial percentage, chose club affiliation as a means of meeting some of their needs. But one applauds a widening approach so that services are available for individuals or groups as they need them without feeling under an obligation to join an organization. The part of the report looking at the needs of the young adult group emphasized the widest possible involvement in the life of the community and the challenge of harnessing their energy and idealism for the benefit of society. It seems unfortunate that in the main recommendations 'clear recognition of adult status' is qualified by the right to have alcoholic drinks in sponsored organizations, for this is neither a sign of being adult nor is it a right in the sense that an organization must provide alcoholic drinks in order to qualify for sponsorship, if by that is meant recognition for grant-aid from central or local government.

The Report endorsed the development of what it called youth work in schools and this can be viewed along several lines:

Clubs and organizations using school premises and facilities but not sponsored by the school:

The school used as a centre (youth or community) for extra-curricular work either for pupils only or for all who wish to avail themselves of the provision: school-wings, being separate provision, but where they are used in conjunction with the total school provision, or part of it: the appointment of a member of the school staff as teacher-leader or youth tutor. The difference in role between these two categories may be that the former has a 50–50 responsibility as a class teacher and club leader, and the latter's function is not so easily or necessarily defined by time and where what he does in school hours is closely related to what he does outside them. Maybe it is too early to assess the problems of these recent developments, but the committee might have tried or recommended that research be carried out. One of the fears at this time was that the Department of Education and Science and the local education authorities were committed to school-based youth work and the teacher-leader appointment to the detriment, at least financially, to other forms of youth work.

Local Education Authorities

The local education authorities are reponsible for providing a youth service in partnership with the voluntary organizations. They are expected to make this provision by drawing up and putting into practice plans for a balanced service in consultation with their voluntary partners. To this end they make available finance in the form of grants for premises and their maintenance, equipment, employment of staff both full time and part-time: the provision of specialist help in the form of organizers, instructors, demonstrators and the use of premises, facilities and equipment on loan. The authorities, in conjunction with the voluntary partners, are responsible for training schemes, development surveys, dissemination of news and information and the provision of area events in which different kinds of youth groups can participate.

The local education committee is an elected body of the councils of counties or county boroughs and the Service of Youth Committee can be either a direct sub-committee of the Education Committee or a sub-committee of the Further Education sub-committee of the Education Committee. (Albemarle recommended that it should be the former.) In many authorities the Service of Youth Committee has co-opted members who are not councillors but who are known to have an interest in or special knowledge of work with young people. Some authorities have established a Youth Advisory Committee made up of interested people and representations of organizations acting with officers to advise the Service of Youth Committee.

Some of the powers of local education authorities are exercised on their behalf in county areas by Excepted Districts or Divisional Executives but neither of these can levy a rate or borrow money. The local authority may develop its own service in that it provides buildings and staff in what has become known as fully-maintained clubs or centres at the same time servicing or offering the services outlined above to units of national organizations or locally sponsored groups. The Youth Service in a local education authority is usually headed by a Youth Service Officer, but this may be a role played by an officer with a wider brief, for instance, Further Education Officer, Youth and Community Officer, with assistants who may be designated as such or as Area Youth Officers or Organizers. Other specialist officers of the local education authority may work closely with the youth officer or their 'specialism' be made available to the Youth Service. These will include such people as the Physical Education Officers, Youth Employment Officers where this service is administered by the local authority, Music Adviser, Art and Crafts Adviser and so on. In large authorities the pattern tends to be towards the division into areas with an Area Youth Organizer enjoying some degree of autonomy as well as being part of a county or county borough service.

Most local authorities have established Leaders' Councils and encourage all units of youth work to send *adult* representatives to a bi-monthly or quarterly meeting. The objects of such councils are the sharing of experiences, discussion of common areas of work with young people, planning and organizing joint projects such as festivals, displays, acts of service, competitions, training and the like. They also afford the opportunity for formulating proposals to the authorities and other bodies and to sharing ideas with workers in other fields of Social work. An off-shoot of the Leaders' Council has been the Area or County or Borough Youth Members' Council where *members* of clubs and organizations meet monthly or bi-monthly to discuss, plan and propose action. This is channelled through the Leaders' Councils or may go direct to the appropriate Service of Youth Committee.

The Voluntary Organizations

The tendency is to think of a non-L.E.A. fully maintained club as being part of a national voluntary organization, but many clubs, voluntary by nature, see their 'parent body' as the local authority's service of youth. They may or may not have taken out an affiliation to the National Association of Youth Clubs or the National Association of Boys' Clubs for example, but they still look to the L.E.A. service for guidance, financial help and the sort of servicing which keeps them ticking-over. In many cases they came into being as a result of developmental work carried out by the officers of the authority and are kept in being by its continued support. Other units are more easily recognized as being part of a national youth organization and only remain in being as long as they continue to function inside the method of work peculiar to that organization, such as Scouts, Guides, Brigades, Y.M.C.A., Y.W.C.A., some of the church groups and Boys' Clubs.

The national youth organization and other organizations with youth work sections like the Churches, have their local, regional or diocesan patterns of committees, with full-time, part-time or voluntary officers, offering some services peculiar to the particular organization. These can be complementary to or duplicating those offered by the local education authority. The Standing Conference of National Voluntary Youth Organizations was founded in 1936 when a number of national youth organizations felt that they had a common aim in encouraging the education of character through leisure time pursuits carried out in an informal atmosphere. Conditions of membership are that the organization shall be a national one with voluntary membership of 10,000 in the age range 10 to 21, promoting the physical, mental and spiritual welfare of its members, be self-governing, determining its own policy and not be connected with any political party. The diversity of approach of the various organizations was recognized as valuable and whilst the objectives are seen as developing the personality of the individual the method could be single-purpose or specialist, for example, training in first-aid. The Conference has a full-time secretariat and besides the bi-annual National Conference local Standing Conferences meet regularly throughout the year and there is co-operation and consultation at central government and local government levels.

Adult (Management) Committees

In general the local education authorities and voluntary organizations encourage the formation of a body of adults to act in a management role to each unit of youth work. Sometimes this is a prerequisite to recognition by the authority or national organization. The purpose of such a committee is to ensure continuity of the unit and answer to the sponsoring body for the way in which the aims and objects of that body are carried out.

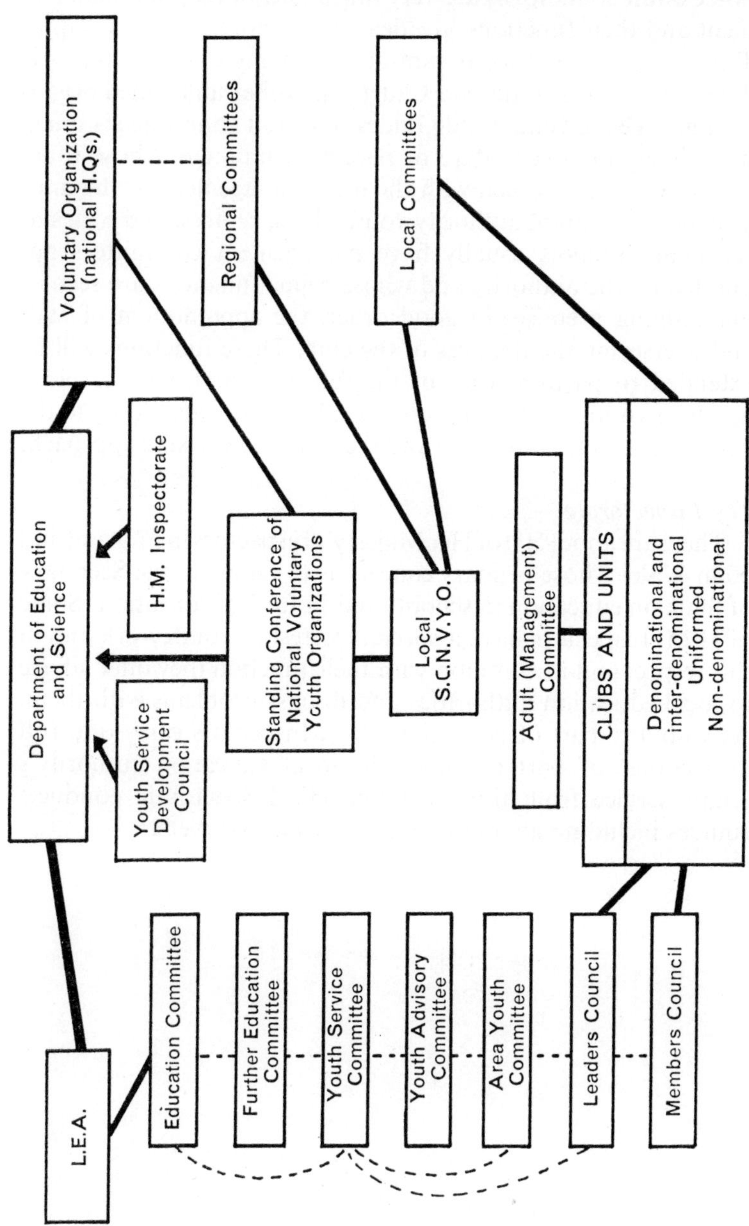
Voluntary Organization
(national H.Qs.)
Regional Committees
Local Committees
Department of Education
and Science
H.M. Inspectorate
Standing Conference of
National Voluntary
Youth Organizations
Local
S.C.N.V.Y.O.
Youth Service
Development
Council
Adult (Management)
Committee
CLUBS AND UNITS
Denominational and
inter-denominational
Uniformed
Non-denominational
L.E.A.
Education Committee
Further Education
Committee
Youth Service
Committee
Youth Advisory
Committee
Area Youth
Committee
Leaders Council
Members Council

Figure 1

Some adult committees are very much part of the total management and their functions are dealt with more fully in Chapter Ten. In the pre-service organizations, Army Cadet Force, Air Training Corps and the Sea Cadets and other uniformed organizations like the Scouts and Guides the adult committee is much more likely to be a welfare or parents' committee whose functions are less concerned with the total management of the unit. The local education authority youth clubs, centres, and wings to secondary schools usually have management committees appointed by the authority and whose prime functions are seen as maintaining premises in good order, the appointment of staff and overseeing the finances of the club. These functions will be extended to pastoral care of the full-time staff, new developments in youth work and professional guidance according to the personnel on the committee and the full-time workers approach.

The Inspectorate

There are about 500 of Her Majesty's Inspectors in England and 50 in Wales whose primary concern is to report to the Secretary of State on education in schools and in further education. Some of H.M. Inspectors have a special interest in youth work and in this respect and in common with their function they offer advice to local education authorities and discuss problems with them. As with any part of education H.M. Inspectors carry out 'full inspections' of part or all of the local education authority's youth service from time to time. The Inspectorate conducts courses including an annual one for youth workers.

Chapter Three

The Young People – Growth Tasks of the Adolescent

As the infant grows he is influenced to learn the ways of his society in order to function effectively in that society. The process whereby we develop from our earliest days to behave, think, feel, react and learn to evaluate things, people and situations in much the same way as those to whom we relate is known as *the socialization process.* This process goes on all our lives and although it is fairly certain that our personalities are moulded, or shaped, in the early years of childhood they are modified and developed by wider social contacts and experiences as we grow. The family is seen as the most formative influence in the life of a child but this must always be viewed in the context of *community* or *society*, for the family acts as a filter through which the norms, values and the influence of other significant agencies, such as school, church, government are passed to the child. As members of a community or society cope with common problems and evolve certain ways of approach such methods become established and form patterns of behaviour. These we call cultures or sub-cultures and they are passed on to succeeding generations. They are attitudinal in that they are organized and consistent, to do with thinking, feeling and acting in relation to other groups, social problems and the general environment. The way of thinking, feeling, and reacting to situations becomes the 'approved' way for *that* society or community and, of course, varies from society to society, from sub-culture to sub-culture. The family's influence on the growing child will depend on the family setting and its characteristics and distinctive design for living which will be greatly influenced by the sub-culture in a complex society like ours. The obvious sub-cultures are social-class, occupational, urban, rural, religious and ethnic. We can enumerate the way the family settings differ, e.g. (1) the emotional content, that is, the love and care that is demonstrated by parents, and particularly the mother, to the children; absence of physical punishment, of threats and of building guilt feelings in the minds of the children: (2) the physical comfort of the home, how the child is nourished and is encouraged to use the home environment positively rather than restrictively, particularly where certain activities result in physical punishment: (3) the intellectual stimulus of the home related to the wealth or paucity of things to enjoy; the use of play time with parents, the demands for responsibility made on the children in terms of tasks they can perform in the home: (4) the handling of conflict, how the parents re-act to the child's aggression and disobedience to them and aggression to siblings or play-mates: (5) the emotional stability of the parents.

Developmental Tasks

'A developmental task is a task which arises at or about a certain period in the life of the individual, successful achievement of which leads to his happiness and to success with later tasks, while failure leads to unhappiness in the individual, disapproval by the society, and difficulty with later tasks.'[1]

These tasks can be viewed as physical, social and intellectual, as coming to terms with the biological growth and change, meeting the needs or demands of society or one's culture and developing a personality in terms of values and philosophy. The notion of *the developmental tasks* is that the time factor determines the stage of the tasks. This can be clearly seen in the biological growth of the individual, for the child learns to walk before he can run, and until he reaches physical maturity there may have appeared some disharmony in the growing body, some organs appearing to develop more rapidly than others, or as in the case of the development of the secondary sex characteristics, to have been arrested awaiting their proper time for development. A task, however, should not be seen as either physical, social or intellectual; for the adjustment to each task is effected by attitudes to the physical, social and intellectual state. A. H. Maslow[2] suggested that the wants, or drives, of man develop in a sequential order as follows:

[1] *HumanDevelopment and Education* – R. J. Havighurst 1953 (Longmans Green & Co.).

[2] *A theory of human motivation* – A. H. Maslow in Psychol. Review (1943).

1. Physiological need to do with the satisfaction of hunger and thirst.
2. Safety needs such as security and order.
3. Love and belongingness needs – affection and identification.
4. Esteem needs, prestige, success, self-respect.
5. Self-fulfilment need.

The first two of these needs can be seen as *survival needs* without which the human organism will die. These needs, then have to be met before the next needs can be met and satisfied and as man develops so the first or 'lower' needs have a less important role in the totality of satisfactions. The needs for acceptance, achievement, success, status, and self-fulfilment become more important and as these are met and according to the degree of self satisfaction and gratification the individual is 'freed' to reach higher potentialities. Deprivation in any part of these developmental or psychological tasks will hinder his personal growth or restrict the possibility of his reaching his potential in a number of human spheres. We can use this as a model in looking at the developmental tasks of adolescence and the socialization process affecting the manner in which these tasks are achieved.

Accepting One's Maleness or Femaleness

At about the twelfth year the child experiences the beginnings of bodily change which will influence physical and psychological development to a marked degree and will set the seal on their maleness or femaleness. This change is known as the pubertal growth cycle and results in the development of secondary sex characteristics. Physical changes begin to distinguish the sexes. The girl begins to take on a more rounded contour, breasts begin to develop, hips broaden and, for many, 'puppy-fat' gives a dumpy appearance; boys become aware of the growth of the genitals, the voice begins to change and both discover the growth of hair around the sexual organs, under the armpits, and the boy begins to sprout facial hair. The body is beginning to prepare itself for its male or female role, in the male, the manufacture of the male sex cells known as spermatozoa (sperm) and, in the female, the manufacture of ova. The female cell, or ova, carries two X chromosomes and the male cell carries both X and

Y chromosomes – the female being produced from the fertilization of two X chromosomes (one from each partner) and the male from one X and one Y.

The sex cells are produced by the gonads being the testes in the male and the ovaries in the female. The former are suspended in the scrotum between the thigh junction and the latter well inside the female body. The male sperms are carried through thin tubes into the body cavity at the groin and join up with the tube running from the bladder to the penis. The penis has three functions, one as an outlet for waste products through urine, erection through stimulus in order to enter the female and thirdly for the emission of semen, the milk-like secretion which carries the sperms. The female egg cells (ova) become active at puberty and at about one monthly intervals an ovum ripens in one of the ovaries and makes its way down to the womb (uterus). During a period of about two weeks the uterus prepares to receive the egg-cell and its walls thicken and produce a number of blood cells. If the egg-cell on its way to the uterus is not fertilized by a sperm cell the ovum dies and the uterus sheds its lining together with the blood-cells and the ovum through the vagina. This is a menstrual flow, or menstruation, and occurs about monthly, the time for the flow lasts about five days. The age at which this first menstrual flow takes place varies from individual to individual and from culture to culture, although it would appear there is less of a variation between climatic zones than was once thought and much more between individuals. Girls may first menstruate as early as 10 years or as late as 20 and the first menstruation is no indication that the regular menstrual flow or cycle has begun and there can be short or lengthy periods of irregularity. Other biological manifestations can affect the regularity of the menstrual cycle, such as tensions caused by anxiety, illness, and emotional upsurges. The discomfort accompanying the menstrual flow is not usually such as prevents young girls leading a normal active life but one has to be aware of the cluster of attitudes surrounding this biological body function. If the child has not been prepared for this by adequate explanation of the physical function, of the purpose, then she may feel guilty or ashamed about the whole process. This could have far-reaching effects on her attitude to the opposite sex, marriage, child-bearing as well as to a whole range of activities both physical and social. Any person, like the youth leader, working with young girls must be aware of both the physical and psychological processes and of the effects of the individual's socialization which might surround the normal biological function with mystery, taboos and shame. He may be a product of similar socialization and find it difficult to help young people for the same reasons that they treat the subject as 'sexy' or not quite nice. Ignorance breeds fear, knowledge liberates us from such fears.

The boy develops a little later than the girl, that is, in comparing the emission of semen with the first menstrual flow as a general rule. The semen has no chemical substance of importance beyond that of carrying the sperm into the female for the fertilization of the female egg. From time to time the male emits semen with or without erotic stimulus. Of itself the emission of semen has no adverse effects. It used to be said that it sapped one's strength but there is no evidence that this is so, but the psychological effects can be damaging unless the young person is helped to understand the function and purpose and any guilt feelings associated with it reduced by significant people, that is, people who are important in the boy's socialization. Often the child's first experience is at night and unexpected. It may or may not be accompanied by an erotic dream of which the child is aware. Sooner or later he will discover that this is not peculiar to him and his peers will talk about 'wet dreams' and undoubtedly some learning goes on because they share common experiences, but if all the learning and understanding is left to this sort of situation it may do little to reduce guilt feeling, at least, because he is not aware that his parents know what is happening to him, or care, or that they think the less said the sooner it goes away. He will be experiencing frequent erections of the penis, not always controllable, and at times embarrassing. This and the emission of semen means that his body is revealing sexual maturity or becoming mature enough to procreate and he needs to be helped to understand this and that as time goes on he will learn how to control this and the accompanying emotions.

In the early adolescent period the young person is most likely to indulge in some form of masturbation and homosexual activity. The young person discovers that certain parts of the body when stimulated give a certain kind of pleasure and, whereas earlier he has enjoyed the discovery of his body for the pleasure this gave, he now discovers a sexual object. But this is not yet attainable in the heterosexual relationship and so he tends to indulge in a fantasy situation where masturbation is the substitute for the sexual act or through sexual play with members of the same sex and age. For the great majority of young people this is a passing phase, is not harmful in itself and should be treated as such by parents and adults working with young people. Again one has to be aware of the psychological effects surrounding such actions and older teenagers, as adults with initiation practices at work, can be very cruel to younger boys at a very emotionally charged period of sexual growth. There is also an awareness that certain parts of the body of members of the opposite sex arouse feelings of pleasure and create physical sensations. How he reacts to this will depend on what he has learned through the help received as he has developed through all the stages of growth, for instance, according to the parents' attitudes to his discovery of his body, the whole process of weaning and the enjoyment he shared with his mother, the attitudes in the home centred round modesty, taboos, the encouragement he was given to ask questions like 'where do babies come from?'

Whilst our present society is more open and frank in its treatment of sexual matters one needs to be aware that for many young people they may not be receiving, through the most influential agencies, that is, those agencies which are concerned with them as total persons, the balance so essential if they are to learn how to handle their developing sexuality as something which is part of the union of body, mind and spirit rather than the ability to indulge in sex acts or events with no more significance than that.

The time of life between 12 and 18 years has been described as the period of male ascendency. At the beginning of this period girls enter the adolescent phase earlier than boys and are bigger and stronger up to about the 13th or 14th year, but then boys grow more rapidly and at the end of the adolescent period are bigger and stronger. Whereas the girl broadens at the hips and puts on fat, the breadth of the boy's shoulders and chest increase, bone and muscle develop and he tends to lose fat. During this time blood pressure increases, the heart rate becomes slower, the normal rate of breathing decreases, more oxygen is made available to exercising muscles which become capable of greater activity. The spurt in strength may not occur at the same time as the spurt in height and the boy is likely to take on the physiological aspect of maturity before he has reached maturity in strength to match his appearance. This may be true of his improvement in co-ordination for this develops at the same time as the strength spurt and being some time later than his height spurt gives the impression that between the two he has become less skilful than he was a few years earlier. More awkward and somewhat clumsy he may be when he is learning to come to terms with his growing limbs at a time when he is also developing a high degree of self-consciousness. The chemical changes taking place in his body in order to facilitate these 'new growths' can effect his attitudes particularly in the activity and social spheres of his life, so that he appears lethargic at one moment and with energy to waste at another, to desire crowd activity alternating with the desire and need to be quiet and alone. This is a time when the boy wants to demonstrate his maleness in terms of strength, skill, and bravery. And this leads to showing off, dare-devil stunts, disregard of safety precautions in activities, demonstrations of endurance and independence.

Coming to Terms with the 'Growing Emotions'

The goal to be achieved is that of emotional or psychological independence, to be able to establish emotional ties to parents and others who have played significant roles in the child's life based on different criteria and to extend such relationships to new acquaintances. The adolescent experiences no new emotions but the child-like emotions become more intensified and diversified, less easy to understand or handle and having deeper and more prolonged effect on the behaviour, not only of the adolescent, but those who are the objects of his passions. If the child is to achieve some degree of independence he needs to go through a period of weaning as important as that experienced in infancy. The changes taking place in the growing organism and the beginnings of an awareness of self, the development of a conscience and the extending range of people with whom he is associating begin to effect his world-view, and result in a challenge of his dependence on others. As the baby making its first solo journey from chair to chair struggles unaided it still looks for the re-assurance that help is available if required and the mother, always ready, knows it has to encourage the child to go it alone, so with the adolescent as he struggles through a period of emotional instability. But whereas in the case of the baby's struggles this is acceptable to adults and seen as an essential for growth, both adults and young people are confused and uncertain about the emotional weaning process. Naturally, the situation is ambivalent. Young people need to become independent beings and crave this state but also require the safety and security of parental, or adult protection. Parents, too, want their children to acquire a marked degree of dependence but enjoy the feeling of being wanted. It seems obvious that young people should challenge first of all that which has given them the greatest security – the challenge is of a complimentary nature and not one of ingratitude.

As with all the developmental tasks of the adolescent the path is made easier at this stage if the socialization process has already laid sound foundations. But even where this has been so the early years of adolescence will demand new approaches for the child's ready acceptance of guidance, and control will give way to a desire not to be controlled and seeing guidance as denying the right to think for oneself or to lead a life of one's own. Many of the controls will be seen as childish, which they are if they maintain the young person in a childlike role. On the other hand the adolescent will be annoyed by the ambivalence when told to 'act his age', meaning be adult, at one moment, and within minutes informed 'he is too big for his boots' inferring that he should not take on an adult role. But in this, as in many other departments of life, the way to lose affection is to be too possessive. Having fitted the child out with a reliable chassis, decent road conditions, a good engine of habits, a safety code of morals, we *must* allow the child to take the journey alone. Emotional maturing must take place and childhood dependencies and ways of life must be abandoned if young people are not to become social liabilities – the eternal Peter Pans.[1] If this task is not achieved the person remains a dependent

[1] *Youth and Youth Groups* – J. MacAlister Brew (revised by J. E. Matthews) Faber.

person, emotionally still a child, and unable to move with an increasing degree of freedom in the adult world.

The rapid social change in our society bringing new recreational habits and mores which the young accept and may create are more difficult for the adult to comprehend. They are seen as a challenge to their way of life and interpreted as rejection of them as persons. Unconsciously parents may resent the freedoms and opportunities their children have, the very freedom of being young, of being acceptable and loved by others, being free of the burden of family. This tends to ways of restricting movement, or, through innuendo or direct comment that the young person 'thinks more of others than his family' and 'dislikes his own home because he spends so much time elsewhere', leading to feelings of guilt and friction. Economic independence is closely related to emotional independence and our society tends to keep the young economically dependent on the home well beyond the stage when, in other areas of growth, he is mature enough to be independent. Economic independence does not appear to depend on the amount of money the young person handles so much as how he receives it. The boy or girl still at school at seventeen may be given an 'adequate' pocket money allowance and it may be equal to or in excess of the amount in the pocket of a friend of the same age who is at work, but the fact of being in receipt of an allowance not earned by being at work can induce a greater feeling of dependency. One questions how young people in a club situation look upon adult's 'kindly' decision to have a lower scale of member-subscription for those still in full-time education. Is this a further way of emphasizing their lack of independence?

At this stage of development the young person turns to other people and situations for emotional satisfactions, most of which, as a child, have been met within the family. Some of these take the form of crushes or hero-worship usually of an adult who takes on all the attributes of an ideal parent or love partner, who is not demanding and on whom affection can be showered, and where any small reciprocal sign, from simple recognition that the young person exists to praise for any act induces a warm emotional state. School teachers, ministers in the church and youth leaders are often the objects for such romantic love. Parents can be most disturbed when they become aware that their young son or daughter appears to be transferring parental-love to another person. The person to whom this is directed may not be aware that he has become the love-object of a young person and, unwittingly but quite naturally, does not react in the way the young person desires and this can produce a form of rebellion which the adult does not understand. Alternatively, the adult may be aware of the 'crush' and use it for his own satisfaction, through pride or desire for power to control another's emotional responses. Workers in these situations should be aware of the methods adopted by young people in their desire for attention, either by being good or troublesome. This should convey some understanding of the problems young people are struggling with in coming to terms with their growing emotions. Support in their emotional crises is one of the tasks of the youth worker no matter how child-like the crisis may seem to the adult, for no matter how 'silly' it appears to the adult it can feel like the ultimate doom to the young person. The youth worker needs to support the home relationships in such situations too. Whether the young person openly criticizes or infers criticism of his parents it serves little purpose if the youth worker appears to support the criticism, but he uses this as an opportunity to talk about their concern although they may express it in what appears to be unacceptable forms at that moment. Usually this is a passing phase in the early years of adolescence but because we believe that most people pass through this stage of growth satisfactorily we should be aware of the opportunities for influence in developing their understanding and control of their emotions or for injuring their peronalities so that we retard their ability to make deeper relationships based on trust.

Developing a Philosophy of Life

The sum of the tasks to be achieved by the adolescent is in personal identity, the desire to be seen by others as an individual unique in his totality no matter how much like others he may be in part. He is set to achieve a set of values drawn from ethical concepts, and a growing moral conscience which marks him out as different to others in the way he views the social scene and reacts to it. The child acquires a set of responses, attitudes, values, motives as a result of social learning in the family and through identification with others. A value is an object or state of affairs which is desired and Havinghurst[1] suggests six ways by which a person comes to desire an object or state of affairs.

1. *Through satisfaction of physiological drives.* The child comes to value food as his hunger drive is satisfied: values activity as it satisfies his drive for physical action: values caressing as caressing satisfies his sex desire.

2. *Through satisfactory emotional experience.* Close to the preceeding method of forming values, for example, the child comes to value other things or states associated with feeding such as warmth, closeness of the mother's body, exploring each other's body during the feeding process. Added to this may be sound, colour, form and line arrangements, rhythms, smells, etc. which induce pleasure for some and displeasure for others. They may be associated in a person's experience with other things and these other things become values, for example, obedience to certain religious rules, sacrifice for patriotic reasons, because they are associated with satisfactory emotional experiences.

3. *Through concrete reward and punishment.* If a person is consistently rewarded for doing certain things, he comes to value those things.

4. *Through association of something with the love or approval of persons whose love and approval is desired.* The reward here is less tangible than that gained in 3 above, more in terms of approval and love.

5. *Through inculcation by someone in authority.* Some learning of values may be through fear or respect of someone in authority, even though there is no reward of love or approval.

6. *Through reasoning or reflective thinking.* Some people learn to reason out some values by analysing behaviour, reflecting on possible consequences and then decide on a desirable course of action.

[1] *Human Development and Education* – R. J. Havinghurst (Longmans) 1953.

Identification is seen as a drive or motive to be like another person. It is through identification with his mother and father that the child acquires the family pattern of behaviour. This is not mere imitation of some physical characteristics but is the acquiring of a duplicate, almost, of the parent in that the child behaves as if he were the parent, reacts and thinks as he believes his parents react and think. As said earlier the parents act as filters of their culture and so through the process of identification the child learns attitudes, ideas, values, taboos, morals appropriate for his cultural group, social class and role in society.[1] This, in the child, is the beginning of conscience. What he sees as right and wrong is really how he sees the parent responding to the situation. As the child grows and he identifies with other significant persons, like school teacher, club leader, neighbours, peers and, maybe, some hero-figure with whom he has no direct contact, he begins to modify the conscience and later as he is able to use reflective thinking he further modifies until he believes that his judgements are his own, though similar to others.

Two features of our modern society appear to have special significance to the adolescent's growth in this respect. One is the need for some source of authority, for any testing of one's identity requires some external approval. But authority is not merely challenged – as it should be – in our society, but debunked in all its forms and certainly not only by young people. Perhaps we have reached the end of an authoritarian age in which attitudes, values and standards can no longer be passed on by the representatives of institutions in a paternalistic and deontological way, but have not yet replaced this with something meaningful to young people, or adults for that matter. This uncertainty will be reflected by parents and the significant others and adds to the confusion facing young people. There is a world of difference beween the situation where young people 'naturally' question values handed-on because they are supported in this by understanding and loving parents, and the situation where parents feel uncertain, insecure and threatened by forces which seem beyond their control. Some of the talk and literature which suggests that the family as an institution has no

[1] *The Psychological Development of the Child* – P. H. Mussen 1964.

meaning in a modern society may not be helpful in the difficult problem of bridging the generation gap.

The other feature, and to some degree its intensity depends on what has just been said, is the identification with the peer group. The young person needs to make his mark in a group, or groups, of his contempories. Much of his understanding of acceptable behaviour will be learned through such affiliation, for here he is unable to claim any rights and the group does not feel responsibility for him as does the family, school or club. This is not to say that the friendship group, or gang, is not possessive, very often it is extremely so, but the young person is not accepted into membership of the gang simply because he is a contemporary or in need of such friendship. The fierce friendships, usually in small groups, at the end of school life give way to more enduring and purposive groupings in the mid-teens. Those adults who work with the twelve to fifteens know how much the friendship groups resemble frog-spawn – separate beings joined by some unseen 'jelly', so that movement by one part pulls all the mass with it. Perhaps in the youth group situation this is more observable with groups of young girls than boys. But soon this breaks up into close friendship of two, three or four with much looser relationships with a number of contemporaries. It is in these sets that a great deal of social learning goes on. The group is able to test itself in many situations which would not be undertaken by the members acting independently, and the challenge of others, adults or groups of young people of a different social class, is handled differently by the group than by the individual. The influence of home, work, similar institutions affecting their individual lives are discussed in the small group settings, they air their grievances and propose their drastic actions and reactions in a way which is well received by their mates and which, it is understood, does not always call for overt action – the hostility being expressed being sufficient release. Sometimes, of course, it leads to overt action, some of it deemed to be anti-social. At an early stage in the adolescent period this being able to compare notes about one's feeling's, how one should respond is particularly relevant to their associations with members of the opposite sex. It is in the small group setting where they discuss what they want from heterosexual relationships, how they should behave with a girlfriend, her expectations and how contemporaries think they should react. In other settings the young person may brag about his conquests, but in the small intimate group it is likely that he has to get nearer to the truth about what really happens when he is on a date. The teen-age peer group has become a powerful influence in the lives of our young people and although there may not be such a thing as a teen-age sub-culture, there is a feeling that one needs to identify with the current youth scene. Styles of dress, music, dance, and certain possessions and ways of conducting oneself are ways in which the individual demonstrates that he belongs to a particular group in society, and not to have any of these means of identification, or not 'going along with' the teen-scene can lead to ostracism by contempories.

On the one hand we observe young people desiring to assume social obligations, to want acceptance from society as full participants, to use their ideals and altruism for the good of society and the development of mankind. On the other hand we see young people appearing to delay the stage at which they accept such responsibilities, not wanting to join the adult world until it is absolutely necessary. These are their struggles in working out a satisfying philosophy of values, ethical concepts and mores which will guide them through their lives.

The Development of Skills – Vocational and Non-vocational

Although his entry to the world of work is delayed until the mid-teens in our society, the adolescent needs to develop skills which enable him to choose an occupation from which he can get certain satisfactions. The preparation for this begins early in his school life in a very general sense and towards the end of this period he is expected to indicate a more specific range of subjects according to ability having a closer relation to the skills required in the occupation of his choice. How real the wide choice of occupations is may be questioned. For many young people parental influence and immediate availability or unavailability of the sort of jobs they feel they would like to do limits choice. The expectations of adults seems to suggest that the school-leaver should be able to make a definite choice of life-long occupation at that age, and the adolescent who moves from occupation to occupation is suspect. Preparation for occupational work is limited for many boys and girls, both in the skills required and adjustment to the new situation. Many jobs require little previous school-based training and the new worker is expected to learn whatever skill is required on the job. Whatever the nature of the job the impression most young people want to give is that it is an important one and that they are good at the skill implied although they do not necessarily see it as total fulfilment in a creative or social sense. They seem more able than many adults to accept the sharp differences between the world of work and the world of leisure. The major parts of the task to be achieved seem to be reaching economic independence and acceptance of worth as an adult. For some young people, of course, a major achievement is to be considered highly competent as a skilled worker and, in this respect, an increasing number of them pursue various kinds of courses, to increase their knowledge and skill which enhances the prospects of promotion.

Increasingly in an industrial society the task of developing skills for an occupation is only part of the need, for as we develop techniques of automation and mass production and work hours are reduced it becomes increasingly important that young people develop skills and interests which will enable them to enjoy and gain satisfactions from the non-vocational part of their lives.

Preparation for Marriage and Family Life

The culmination of achievement of the developmental tasks for the majority of adolescents is the desire to 'break-away' from the family group and to create a new family unit. Another choice to be made, then, is that of a partner in order to set up a home and have children of one's own. Quite early in the adolescent period the process began with the tentative and self-conscious play between members of the sexes, usually in large groups where the boys show off their masculinity and the girls group together to be impressed by this display. There is a period of sexual-effectiveness display before courtship begins, some of which is classified as horseplay or fooling-about, and appearing crude to the adult. At this stage the young people have not yet learned how to handle this communication in a more sophisticated and mature way for they are only a short step away from the stage of childhood when members of the opposite sex were not seen as objects of the sexual drive, and so much of their display is in the form of physical play, chasing, pushing, scrummaging, snatching possessions and enjoying the struggle of retrieving them. The next stage is less robust but still in groups of four or six with degrees of flirtation acceptable to all in the group before the courtship stage is entered. Whilst there is more social mobility at present most partners are selected from the same social class and this and the sub-culture are influential in mate-selection. Young people's attitudes towards marriage are undoubtedly influenced by their experiences at home and, to a lesser degree, of their contemporaries. Career prospects and the adult role they are expected to play also affect how soon they can enter the courtship and marriage state. This is coupled, to some extent, to economic independence but probably more to what the partners believe is essential in material terms for the establishment of a home. Some young people give the impression that marriage is being 'tied down', meaning the end of freedom and a complete break with friends and a particular pattern of life, others look forward to it as the fulfilment of all that is desired in a relationship, and yet others enter it as a matter of course.

Marriage and family have different forms in different societies and in our society monogamy and institutional marriage are the accepted forms. The changes brought about in the last half century have seen the extended family give way to what is called the nuclear family with changing influence on the off-springs of such marriages. There is little evidence to show that it is any the less stable than previously.

The Young and Present Society – Too Many Choices?

Hansjurgen Schubert writing in *Die Zeit* (June 1970) says 'Not too little but rather too much is in their (young people) power to decide. In contrast with a lack of opportunity to participate in decisions at school or at work, they have otherwise an unprecedented amount of freedom of choice. Hobbies, job, travel, pleasure, partners, and the possibility of early sex experience – create agony of choice. The welfare state provides security even for those who fight most vehemently against it. Wars and disasters, the stern wardens of earlier generations, no longer limit people's opportunities. Almost, everything is available or can be obtained with a little extra effort. The way is short from abundance to satiety.'

They have too much – and yet too little of the most important things: credible examples to follow and inspiring short term objectives. The parent generation of hard-working home builders has forgotten to leave some tasks for their children which demand total involvement. This omission is one we shall all pay dearly for.

What remains then? For most young people the way of least resistance they adapt. Within the group they demonstrate their allegiance by carefully planned unity in dress and attitudes, copying formulations and new concepts. They practise a new type of fellow-travelling in the belief that they are attacking old orders, they do a bit of provoking here, a bit of demonstrating there. But at the same time, whenever there is advantage in it, they dip into the overflowing bowl of the abundant society.

Primitive man had simple choices. They were basically ones of survival or extinction within a clearly circumscribed society. Modern society is reached through a long process of making choices and in this creating more choices for more people. As society has created opportunities for young people to extend their childhood, or delay their entry into adulthood, and seen a period between the two as having its own phases of development so the initiation-type ceremony of the primitive society, when the child passed into adulthood in a day, has become drawn out over six or seven years. His preparation for a definite adult role in his society is diffuse and the role he plays during the adolescent period uncertain. In childhood, the family is an intimate source of reference: in adulthood the source of reference is society. But the adolescent is in between these two points of reference and the claims of the adult society are about to be made – he is leaving or, has left, the claims he made on the family as a child. Needing a source of reference he turns to the other young people in like situations and as important as his peer group is to him it is unable to provide the experience of the family or the authority of society. This at a time when so many choices have to be made – choices which affect the whole of one's life. It has been said that 'the choice of role is choice of identity' and the young person is busy in the role choice at a time in his life when he is being exhorted, pursuaded and seduced by many voices but with uncertain sources for reference. The intense awareness of self results in a desire to *feel* that things are right and he is somewhat dismayed at the lack of passion or detachment with which adults hold their beliefs and values. They are severely practical in the way they express their feelings and being able to make a choice, to do something, is more important than the choice they make. If they feel that a thing is right they want to get on with the action. They are torn by the apparent hypocrisy of adults, by the divisions within society, and even the divisions within the institutions of society. An example of this is the unhelpful way society reacts to their developing sexuality as though adults, and particularly those significant adults like parents, youth workers, teachers are unaware of the change in every relationship which ensues from the development of the secondary sex characteristics. In this, as in a number of other choices, he is exhorted on the one hand to delay the desire for immediate pleasure for something more desirable later and, on the other, if he must satisfy his desires now, to exercise caution by using modern methods of contraception.

The following passage is a translation of a pamphlet by an Austrian 'Teddy Boy', found in a youth camp in the late fifties, and obviously written as a challenge to adult society. Linguistically it is a play on the meaning 'halbstark', the German equivalent to Teddy Boy, meaning half-strong, half-baked, a youth pretending to be an adult but not quite making it. It was a label of rejection used against the young generation.

To the weak – by an unknown 'Halfstrong'. Because you are weak, you have called us 'Halfstrong'; and by doing so you are condemning a whole generation against whom you have been sinning because you are weak. We have given you two decades to make us strong, strong in love and strong in goodwill, but you have made us halfstrong, because you are weak.

Your uncertain 'no' was not firm but weak: as children we had only to demand things by screaming for them and you said 'yes', to spare your poor nerves, and you called that 'love'!

Because you are weak you bought peace from us, while we were small, with money for the pictures and ice cream: you were not doing that for our sake but for yourselves and for your comfort, because your hope and faith are weak.

We are halfstrong and our souls are even less strong than we are; we are causing noisy disturbances, because we don't want to cry out for all those things you didn't teach us!

We know how to do sums and to read, and we are taught how to count petals of nice little flowers; and we know how the foxes live. We have also learnt how to sit still and put up our hands, but there are no little flowers in the big cities, and no foxes, and how to meet life? – that you did not teach us.

We would even like to believe in God, a very strong one who understands everything and who wants that we are good. But you have not shown us human beings who are good because they believe in God. You are worshipping money, and murmur, like prayers, the results of the football pools.

Put away your pistol, Inspector, and tell us what is worth doing. Do you really love that order which you are serving, or do you only love your right to a salary and a good pension? Show us, whether you are strong as a human being. How many good deeds are you committing secretly, as a Christian?

We are noisy and cause a public disturbance, but you are all fighting behind people's backs, mercilessly, one against the other. You are intriguing against each other for better paid posts. Are we not the distorted mirrors of your sham existence? For each one of us who is noisy, show us one amongst you who is silently good. Instead of threatening us with batons, confront us with men who can show us the way: not with words but with their lives. But you are weak; the strong ones go to Africa and are Negroes – because they despise you as we do.

For you are weak, and we are halfstrong!

The recording below gives insight of the range of complexity in the daily life of a young person. The 'story' was told to a student in training for full-time leadership and is printed as he recorded it. Introducing the recording the student explained that the young person was known to him and understood the purpose of the student's exercise. The student set the scene by saying the young man was 18 years of age, was working in a shoe factory having left a secondary modern school at 15, lived on a large council estate in a Midland town and the father had been in the shoe industry all his working life. He headed the recording:

A Day in the Life of John

7 a.m. he wakes, without the alarm-clock ringing as he wakes automatically now; he looks round at the room – untidy as usual because of his 'kid' brother Bob (two years younger), feelings of resentment at no privacy in life – didn't feel like work, started to go back to sleep – Mum's entry, her telling him he can't have time off because the Old Man's ill and he's the only one at work – rush to the bathroom, older sister in already, good-natured shouting at each other. Before leaving he realized he didn't have enough money; had to ask mum, yet he earned £8 per week – how embarrassed he felt! Waiting at bus stop, friends go by on scooters; how he'd have one soon; feelings of resentment against his dad for being ill, still he was used to that by now. He started to daydream about Friday and Saturday nights' dances, the only laughs in the week. He also thought about the holiday he was trying to save for, it would be useless going if he only had a few quid to spend, what would his mates say. There's that gorgeous girl again, by God he didn't arf feel scruffy in his working clothes. Still it all washed out during the evenings and weekends, and she wasn't a snob. His bus companion was a workmate, Bert, about 45, he's always moaning about the 'bloody' government. How 'Arold's making a bigger mess every day.' He didn't know much about politics, except that his dad liked Harold, and that his mum didn't care; he tried to say that he thought that he (Harold) was making the best of a difficult job, but Bert wouldn't give him a chance to finish. They went separate ways at the end of the journey, as Bert was in a different part of the factory for the week. He moaned about 'them' not caring what he wanted to do, he'd been on that small hand-press for two years now and didn't want to move. Yet John remembered him moaning almost non-stop about how boring that hand-press job was. Just what did Bert want out of life: what in fact did John himself want out of life, he certainly didn't want to end up like Bert, forever moaning at everything; yet what was there for him at the factory; his dad had fixed the job for him and he had stuck it for 3 years so far. He thought again of evening classes, but who would tell him what to study or how to go about joining the classes.

As he wandered on, head down in thought, he saw a blue flash in the gutter, stooping down he found a £5 note. Marvellous!

What a great night he could have on Saturday, he was already seeing the beer and the whisky and girls around him, when he remembered mum – 'Give it to the police' she would say, his sister would agree. His dad? – probably a sly wink and £2 10s. each. Ask the Foreman, he thought; on arriving at work he did, 'Put it in your pocket, son', he said. John thought that the best idea as no one would miss it, yet he kept hearing his mum say 'Hand it in at the police station'. He resolved to discuss it at tea break, he was the only boy in their group so they could give him advice, he thought. During the tea break, when he brought the subject up, about half the group said if they found any money they would spend it, a couple said 'give it to the police', some said they would keep half and give half in, one said he would hand it in to a police station miles from where he found it, so he could claim it in a month. One tried to make him give him the £5 note saying he would turn it in for him! John felt no nearer to solving the problem and decided to hand it in to the police station.

During the afternoon he was working with Eric, aged about 30. He enjoyed working with him, as he always seemed to be interested in what John said about things. They discussed many things from cars to girls, and John felt good being able to talk freely to someone who didn't criticize everything he said. Eric's philosophy of life seemed to be 'live and let live'. John felt this would suit him, but he couldn't understand how Eric could be so placid over big issues in life like politics, bosses, authority, blokes he didn't like, and parents, etc. This was one of John's big problems; he felt so much for them, yet everything he said seemed to provoke mum and dad into shouting at him. The fellows at work said 'enjoy yourself while you're young', telling vivid stories of their drink-ups and women in their youth, and swearing with every other word. When he did stay out with the boys, had a few drinks perhaps, or got home late, or let a few swear words slip out, either mum or dad would go mad; keeping on about what the neighbours would say if he got into trouble with the police – couldn't they just trust him?

During the afternoon tea break someone mentioned religion, and some of the men got very agitated: 'The church is only for the rich', 'How can there be a God if he lets people be tortured in P.o.W. camps', 'Church-goers are all hypocrites, getting all dressed up to go to church on Sundays, then getting boozed in the evenings'. These were the sort of things he always heard, and usually always from the same crowd. The quiet fellows, whose views he would like to hear, never expressed themselves loudly. He thought again of mum dressing up for church on Sundays, of her moaning at dad for not going; his sister always asked John to go, but he could refuse her easily. He was grateful his mum had decided that he need only go to church when he wanted to. He could only think of Jesus as a kindly old man with a beard, patting people on the head as if they were little children. Then he thought of the local vicar who always treated him like a little boy – didn't he know he was 18 now! He realized there must be something in religion, there were too many people using it for it to be unimportant, but how could he feel anything for that weak flabby-fleshed vicar. No! – religion could wait till he had enjoyed himself.

When he arrived home, he told mum about the £5 note. She was in a bad mood and shouted, 'You should have kept it, you know how much we need it.' He was on the verge of shouting at her when he realized that it had been his choice about going to the police, and not hers. He told her he would probably get it back after a month, if no one claimed it – he felt pleased that he had avoided a row.

Although he had a little money left, he was determined to go out tonight; it had been a frustrating day and the thought of T.V. nauseated him. He was feeling a bit lost at the moment; his mum was talking to Bob – she always seemed more interested in him, and his sister was working late; so he turned the record player up at full volume to stop himself thinking and getting morbid. His mum must be in a good mood tonight as she didn't yell at him to turn it off. About 7.30 he started to get changed; an almost immediate cue for his 'kid' brother to start talking to him and driving him mad with his stupid questions about his girls, friends and work. He felt good tonight as he was going out soon, so he was friendly towards him and didn't tell him to clear off. As he was leaving, his mum shouted 'Don't be late again'; he knew by now that on Thursdays she went over to her sister's and wouldn't be in till nearly midnight, so it wouldn't matter what time he got in. On other nights when she stayed in, and could worry about him all night, even 10 o'clock could be late!

He went into town to the local coffee bar. All the gang were there, Sam, 16, Mick, 16, both still at school: Alan, 17, Tony 17½, both at work, with scooters; Ian, 18, still at school but owned a scooter, and John. Even though he had no transport, he was the oldest and earned the most, so he was usually the leader in many things. He enjoyed this feeling of being 'in' with a group and completely relaxed in the evenings. Tonight they just wanted to sit and talk, making their 'cokes' last for ages. Someone did suggest they went down to the Youth Centre which they had joined for something to do during the week, but they hadn't been for 4 weeks and knew that they couldn't get in without paying back subs. They were nearly all broke so they stayed in the coffee bar till 10.30 then went home.[1].

Influences on decision-making

Girls prepare for a very different adult role than do boys, centred on home-making and family compared with occupational performance. Despite the fact that girls will enter occupations and develop certain occupational skills and may wish to continue in employment after marriage the strength of future or forward planning is in the occupations or roles around marriage, home and family, whereas the future planning of the boy is centred firstly around work occupations. This is in line with the expectance of the male to be seen as the main source of provision for the family and that of the female to manage, and to a large degree, control how resources are used in the home to meet the needs of the family. Daniel Solomon[2] carried out a study of the influence process as it relates to decision-making by investigating both the relevant situational factors impingeing on the deciding individual, and certain stable characteristics of his personality with which the situational forces are believed to interact. The sample of the study consisted of American adolescents and the sources of influence most likely to be of importance in most decisions of these young people it was assumed were

[1] I am indebted to W. Lorryman for the use of this recording, made whilst he was a student at the National College for the Training of Youth Leaders 1966–67.

[2] Influences on the Decisions of Adolescents – Daniel Solomon – in *Human Relations*, a quarterly journal of studies towards the integration of the social services, 1963.

parents, peers, impulses and values. The strength of a single source of influence will depend on the *direction* of influence, i.e. the decision that has to be taken in terms of choice to do something or refrain from doing: *the intensity* with which the influence is exerted i.e. vociferousness; incentives, used in the external sense and the degrees to which a given impulse or value is activated – feelings, desires; and the *power* of the influence – source, i.e. how the decision-maker is orientated towards accepting influence from that source, independent of the situation. From the analysis of the power scores for each source of influence (parents, peers, impulse and value), parents and values received greater mean scores than did impulses and peers; girls showed greater mean power scores than did boys for each influence source; girls appear to be generally more receptive to influence, whatever its source. The difference in receptivity to influence between boys and girls can be correlated with the greater need for independence expressed by boys than that expressed by girls. This has a bearing on the adult roles they expect to fulfil. Girls showed stronger orientation towards the influence of their peers than did boys. Solomon suggests that, perhaps as girls approach the period in which they will be placed on their own resources, they temporarily increase their reassuring dependence upon one another in order to feel more certain of their competence and endowments for the future roles. Parents tend to feel a greater need to be protective of their daughters than of their sons, particularly in adolescence, and, in part the dependence which this protection affords may be an appropriate forerunner to the dependence on a husband she will be expected to maintain. Girls appear to have more powerful values than do boys and this is possibly because values are instilled into girls more strongly by their parents due to their greater protective concern about conduct; they may, therefore, learn to place greater reliance and emphasis on the influences of their own values. A 'good reputation' is widely perceived by girls to be an important requirement for attracting a desirable husband. At the same time, in order, to appear 'feminine' young women may strive to live up to a stereotype which expects women to be less intelligent, less rational, more emotional and unreasonable ('female logic'), more changeable (the women's prerogative), less competent in certain areas (women drivers) than men. It may be that culturally the male is encouraged to develop intellectual powers and dextrous skills in order to be successful and the female to minimize these in order to compete effectively for a desirable husband. At a later stage we shall look at what this means in terms of the girls' needs and how these may be partly met in the mixed youth group.

Social Class and Personality

Our interest in social class comes from the fact that social class significantly determines the social environment of the individual.[1] As we have seen the child learns the ways of society as they are represented to him by his family in the first instance and then by other significant people and institutions like school, church, neighbours, peers, clubs, etc. but again, he is heavily influenced by how his parents see those other influences and the value they put on their roles. Despite the talk of, and to some degree the opportunities for, social mobility most people live in neighbourhoods which can be defined in social class terms, that is, a tendency to live in social areas for the most part made up of people who do similar work and have similar ways of thinking and feeling about things. Such a system determines the wants and goals of individuals in that environment and influences the way these are met. They have their own cultural and social barriers which inhibit, if not prevent, total social intermixing. The important meaning for the youth worker is to understand how social class creates different learning environments for children of different classes. At the same time care has to be exercised in implying value-judgements when assigning 'goods' and 'bads' to the classifications of working-class, middle-class, upper-class environments.

Although the extent of the enduring consequences of early child-rearing practices have not been clearly established, there is evidence to justify the theory that mother-child relationships influence the immediate and subsequent behaviour of the child. Child-rearing practices are sub-culturally bound to a large extent and it has shown that in the lower working-class situation

[1] *Individual in Society*–Krech, Crutchfield and Ballachey (McGraw Hill), 1962.

it is more likely that the child is fed on demand rather than at prescribed times and that this indiscriminate feeding continues as the child grows, helping himself to food, often eating standing-up, whereas the middle-class attitude leads to the child eating at certain times mostly with members of the family at the meal-table. This immediate or delayed gratification is in line with a number of other practices which induce the same trait of choosing between the immediate, if small, reward, and the delayed and greater reward. However, in some working class environments, the child is handled more often by the mother and siblings and is more likely to sleep with the mother or siblings in the same bed than is the child of the middle-class or upper-class family. This appears to encourage strong family ties but may also lead to greater dependency on others and later the parents may experience difficulty in 'weaning' the young boy or girl away from the need for physical proximity to sleeping alone. It is still possible to find adolescents who are afraid to sleep alone – this being an experience they have not yet had. The home situation where there is a strong maternal tie with the child in those families where the marital roles are still clearly defined in terms of the male's external occupation, meaning he plays little part in the upbringing of the children, there is a greater dependence on the mother and, as she relies on an unrational (to the child) mixture of indulgence and punishment, this can produce emotional insecurity which, in later life, results in the child's inability to take responsibility. The role of the father may take one of two courses. Because he feels a loss of status in the work situation, where he is dominated and submissive to processes which take away initiative and reduce dignity, he may abrogate his duties as a father in the home situation or become domineering and punitive. The mother reacts to whichever role the father plays and either takes on his role as well as her own in dealing with the children or uses threats of 'wait until your father comes home'. In either case there is a distortion of roles leading to emotional insecurity. The child, as he grows develops techniques to protect himself, or gain rewards from the mother; the father is tolerated or seen as a severely punitive person from whom early escape is sought.

The middle-class approach – and perhaps the upper working-class aspires to middle-class approaches – to child rearing may be more consistent with those values of independence, rationalization, delaying gratifications and enabling the child to gain a helpful time-concept. It is likely that the marital roles are less sharply defined and the father takes on certain functions in the home, sometimes with the mother, sometimes alone, which previously were seen as solely the women's. Here the father's status in the occupational role may be less submissive and he feels less threat to his masculinity when he shares domestic roles with the mother. The atmosphere, physical comfort and amenities of the home also varies and affect the socialization of the child. Naturally the parents' attitude to such institutions as school and church will determine to a large extent the attitude of the child to such institutions and the degree of help they will get from them. 'In spite of increased social mobility and the fact that the upper strata of the working-class are increasingly developing middle-class attitudes and aspirations, it remains true that for the lower strata of the working-class a distinctive cultural heritage places them at a disadvantage in the educational system. . . . The sense of separation from the middle-class culture of the school is reinforced continuously, by the indifference and hostility to education which characterizes certain lower working-class communities.' This, in terms of reaction to discipline, attendance, competition, subsequent rewards, by the middle-class and lower working-class children, as much as the intellectual content, he brings to his school experiences. If the middle and upper working-classes put great store on achievement at school and reinforce this in numerous ways, at home and through involvement in parent-school type functions, 'the lower working-class parent and child have no reason to assume that the value of education is self-evident, for the lower working-class occupational and cultural life does not allow for the essentially middle-class values enshrined in education. For lower working-class people the opportunities for social mobility are negligible and the school is the symbol of a competition in which they do not believe they can succeed'.[1] The general features of the home and neighbourhood and the attitudes of parents gather greater

[1] *Sociology in Social Work* – Peter Leonard – Routledge & Kegan Paul 1966.

significance and exert more influence as the child grows. Evidence shows that homes where there is a degree of permissiveness, consultations about decisions, conversations between children and parents, within a warm atmosphere and a strong emotional support of the children, are more likely to produce children who demonstrate leadership, assertiveness, outgoingness and playfulness. They show more curiosity and constructiveness, are more nonconforming and disobedient, meaning they are able to express feelings and emotions including protests against authority, than children brought up in more 'controlled' homes with many clear cut rules and restrictions who tend to be quiet, well-behaved, shy, socially unassertive, highly conforming and lacking in curiosity and creativity.

The implications for the youth worker are the recognition of the influence of the sub-cultural values on young people, so that he may be able to interpret behaviour and understand the underlying reasons: to recognize his own cultural values and how much at conflict these may be with some of his members: in trying to help individuals to recognize the problems of communication he may experience and not expect certain actions which are a normal part of his experiences to be possible for others (for instance, it may be extremely naïve to say 'haven't you talked this through with your father', or to think that withdrawal of privileges will have the same effect on some of his members as they would to him): to recognize that success in activities may be all important to some but that others will not participate because the risk of failure is too great; that some will seek attention through ways which he thinks childish or unacceptable; that there will be conflict between young people who bring into the club situation different values and norms reflecting their different socialization.

With this sort of study we can look at the purpose of youth work and the role of the youth worker.

Chapter Four

The Purpose of Modern Youth Work

'The motives of those who first sought to fill adolescent leisure were mixed and at least unconsciously self-interested. Ensuring that the young grew into "full Christian manliness", together with training them to be "good citizens" and for "responsible roles in society" all involved preparing the young to accept an economic, political and religious structure because it was there and because any radical disturbance of it would have endangered the power of those who controlled it. These arc intentions which have been given persistent repetition since. Drawing out latent but respectable forms of such qualities as leadership and initiative has rarely, even since the nineteenth century, taken account of the fact that they can often be well expressed and experienced when their goal is criticism of extablished order. Instead, youthful rebellion, however expressed, has continued to be taken as evidence either of an understandable but naïve and passing idealism or of a deep seated maladjustment to existing society. The providers cannot usually be accused of evil intent: they have nearly always been in positions of social responsibility and blinkered by their own experience. It has been almost inevitable that they would unconsciously pass on to their clients the assumption that "worthwhile" pursuits are only those sanctioned within the areas of society in which the providers themselves habitually move. Youth work has often become far less a means of developing young people than of unintentionally restraining and repressing them.'[1]

Much of the earlier youth work was model-centred, that is, that 'good' or acceptable social development with certain prescribed virtues was what was seen in the person who offered himself as leader to a group of young people, and he became the

[1] *The Social Education of the Adolescent* – Davies and Gibson OUP (Ibid).

model on which the young were to fashion themselves. As much leadership was undertaken by those in a more privileged group the sorts of experiences they had and the values inherent in the institutions to which they belonged, or had attended, became the yardstick by which progress in the young person's development was measured. For instance terms associated with public-school life and 'the gentility' appeared regularly in the aims and objects of the early youth groups. 'We believe strongly that the lads can appreciate and will learn for themselves that subtle something which is called "good form", which is such an important factor among the higher classes' (St. Christopher's Working Boys Club, London). Words like 'to become Christian gentlemen' – even a qualification to being Christian! – 'team spirit', 'worthwhile pursuits', 'good manners', 'upright, sober and an honest worker' were reflections of what was seen as the model epitomized by the leader and therefore desirable for the young people.

Leisure time was seen as something to be used for improvement in the direction of such virtues and not to be wasted on pursuits which may be pleasurable to the young person. But, as MacAlister Brew says 'this is not exclusive to youth work before 1939. Members of education committees, even teachers and local authority officials, who should know better, are still suspicious of a service to young people which supplies nothing but what they like to call "mere amusement" – though why it should be less worthy to make people happy than it is to inoculate them with doses of ill-digested information, it is difficult to discover'. One might add not only in education, for the Church has been equally at fault in this. And not only before 1939 but, to a fair degree, to the present moment.

In the previous chapter it was suggested that the youth worker can learn about the young people who use the organization in a number of ways, or parts. The human sciences offer help in looking at the development of man, at particular stages of human growth, at society in general and its divisions in terms of class, culture, structure and organization and the effects of these on people. Through such knowledge the student may perceive purpose for his work with young people in a generalized sense and then in particular, through an organization. For some young people, if the model-centred approach to youth work has been the way the leader has worked in the past, there is a need now for the approach to be much more 'client-centred', that is where their state, their environment, their needs are paramount. The definition of socialization, 'learning the ways of society in order to function effectively within it', does not mean that we help young people to develop in order to fit into present society, where conformity is seen as the only desirable state, nor inducing them to fashion themselves in a mould which alienates them from their background. In a delightful book designed as a dialogue between a questioner and the author broadening the questions and commenting on them, John Brennan[1] says 'Parents who have struggled to bring up their families undoubtedly feel demoralized by the youngster who almost repudiates his family and ignores most of its standards as soon as he gains the freedom produced by having a job of his own'.

Can this situation be avoided, if as you say, we are likely to see young people advancing and developing quicker? Briefly, yes. It can be done through a school which sees 'responsibility', as part of its curriculum, and which can tackle family life and modern social history in its final year syllabus. It can be done by the youth worker who encourages responsibility and, incidentally, this is not the same thing as conformity. Too many youth workers think of nonconformity as irresponsibility. Responsibility can be exercised in the most 'way-out' project.

Defining purpose is a philosophical exercise and an exercise of faith. Too often the desire to express purpose becomes confused with method and the danger is that desired ends are seen as being achieved only through certain approaches. The ends, whatever they are, may not be achieved by the method in any case and there is little insight in assuming that if one method does not work, no other method will achieve the desired ends. In many situations such an approach has led to a 'wrong' attitude to human activity, for example, as many young people are probably 'put-off' Shakespeare because they are compelled to learn whole passages to repeat parrot fashion as are introduced to the wonders

[1] *Thinking about Young People* – John Brennan – Pergamon Press 1969 (75 pages).

of his works, as many see mountains and the countryside only as a challenge as part of some scheme and avoid them, as are introduced to their beauty to be simply enjoyed. The educator, social worker, youth worker and, certainly the Christian should not need reminding of the uniqueness of the person and of his value as an individual. Such a worker must believe that each person is capable of growth towards greater social sensitivity and responsibility and that each person has underdeveloped abilities in creativity, originality and leadership. He must believe that the child desires its own share in the becoming of things: it wants to be the subject of the event of production.[1] These abilities seem to emerge and grow when people work together. What Buber calls 'sharing in an undertaking and entering into mutuality'. Within this sharing of an experience with his fellows there will be conflicts reflecting their individual and small group uniqueness for no matter how similar they may be in many aspects, age, sex, background, as soon as they feel released from the conformity that says all of you do this in this fashion, then from their unique position they will produce, or desire to produce, something different. The conflicts, handled with skill, can be used creatively not to produce a compromise for the sake of peace, but to enable growth towards a set of values which are the stronger because they reach them themselves. The pronouncement by someone having authority because he has reached his set of values will bring hostility, anguish or resignation – how often we deny the growing experiences we have had, to others. Whatever the setting, and there is no reason within a youth service why there should not be a great variety, the adolescent will only accept the influence of the youth worker through his confidence in that person. This confidence is only attained when the client becomes aware that the worker is not making business out of him but accepts him as he is, and what he can become, is desirous of taking part in his life but on the terms directed by the client, and where there is mutual trust.

If earlier youth workers were guided by their values, interpreted in the way mentioned, giving rise to a prescriptive model and we now see these as unsuitable as a modern approach then

[1] *Between Man and Man* – Martin Buber – Fontan Library, 1961 (Chapter 111).

the present youth worker needs to have another set of guiding principles which help to direct him and against which he can evaluate his work. Some of these principles will be suggested in the following chapter.

'I had six white mice. . . . . They had one of these little treadmills they used to run round and round and round on. It used to tickle me. They never used to get tired of it. I'd have got fed up with that, you know, walking round and round. They didn't get fed up with it, but there's no purpose in it, is there?'

'You must get something out of life, or otherwise you wouldn't live it, would you? You'd do away with yourself if you got nothing whatever out of it. If you didn't get something out of life you'd get so miserable you wouldn't want to live. You'd just lose the will to live.'[1]

What is the something that one must get out of life? Is it the same for all? Or is this the same question as what is man's destiny? The youth worker must believe that he is engaged in a relationship which enables young people to discover the something that one must get out of life. But he also believes that some forms of life are better than others, that health is preferred to sickness, education to ignorance, freedom to bondage. He is concerned not only with helping to meet the immediate goals but also in helping the young person to participate in change, to be instrumental in a community of work in bringing about change and to be ready to face the consequences of change. In this he believes that young people should have access to adult guidance or council and are not abandoned because outwardly they appear to have moved from the child-state to adult-state.

Whatever it is that the young person seeks from life is not obtainable from one source only although one sort of experience may very much influence the way he achieves it, and possibly the way he evaluates it. In more recent years the central government, local education authorities and the national youth organizations have extended their range of work beyond the 'orthodox' club, centre, settlement to work with spontaneous groups, special groups and the so-called 'unattached'. They are beginning to see that the Youth Service can *offer* opportunities

[1] *Portrait of a Young Girl* – Pauline Smith and Brian Blake – Hutchinson 1965.

for some young people who may not wish to belong to a membership organization. These opportunities include counselling services, information centres, café-clubs, 'drop-ins', etc., and the opportunity for *any* young person to take advantage of any scheme organized centrally by the authority, the organization or national body, without having first to be a registered and, therefore, sponsored member of a 'recognized' club or unit. A further development perhaps of greater significance is the move to relate the youth service to the community and, beyond that, to see youth work community oriented. The second seems a natural progression from the first. Whilst the Youth Service was a self-contained service of organizations and clubs it could exist by creating its own regulations about which group and which individuals qualified for recognition and help, by building an 'ethos' of its own which justified its regulations about recognition. But when it moves out of this sort of structure to carry its resources to young people who can benefit from them without having to 'belong to the system' then it is moving into a community oriented situation. It is beginning to see the needs of young people as the needs of a total community, that they may be met through a variety of provision and techniques which does not separate out either the problems or the young people from the rest of their community experiences in order to 'treat' them.

Still by far the majority of youth clubs and other units of youth organizations are 'led' by voluntary workers as distinct from those which have a full-time 'professional' leader. The former, in terms of leader-member contact time, range from one night per week meetings to five nights per week. They come into being from a variety of causes and for a variety of purposes. It may well be that a group of young people express a desire to have a club – to want to meet together for either specific activities or for more general social purposes, or some individual adult or sponsoring body feels that there should be a club for young people in a particular locality. Sometimes parents express a wish for some kind of youth organization for their children and approach the school, the church, or other agency, with a view to that body taking on the responsibility for the group. The reasons are not always explicit but there is an underlying belief that young people need, and like, to have this sort of experience and, in the main, it is seen in 'good' terms. This seems to suggest that under wise leadership and encouragement young people can strengthen the better in themselves and become fuller persons. Without this sort of article of faith the practice would be meaningless. It has to be a belief that people will respond to appeals for altruism as well as to appeals to selfishness. And whereas the selfish need may be seen to be being met in the short term, altruism may not manifest itself for some time to come. Assessing human betterment, measuring human achievement is a difficult enough occupation at all stages of growth and certainly one which the youth worker understands but he is pushed to demonstrate it by many individuals and groups in society. Too often he feels a need to justify social education by programme content, and even in this there is almost a league-table of activities where some, drama, music (of a certain type) art, members' committee, are seen to have intrinsic value whilst table-tennis – in this context disparagingly called ping-pong – 'just sitting and chatting', moving to beat music, receive low value and are at the bottom of the league, if not relegated to the second division! There may be a danger that the appeals to the young people's altruism to participate in some scheme of social service as part of the club's programme overlooks the need for such a service to be given within the home. As John Brennan says 'It's rather peculiar to me that the idea of service seems to preclude one's own family.'[1] Of course it is more exciting to be part of such a scheme and obviously there is a need to help people to be aware of other's people's needs and to encourage participation in meeting them, but to be too busy helping other's and neglecting one's own may be running away from reality – another form of escapism.

Whatever the setting in which young people meet within the Youth Service influence is seen as an essential element. Still, this influence is seen personified and, in the large area of voluntary and localized units, by an adult or adults who belong to the sponsoring agency, like the Church, or selected by the agency for some special attributes. In a few cases such a person may be selected or nominated by young people themselves. If such persons are to become social educators there are two concepts

[1] *Thinking about young people* – John Brennan (ibid).

of self and of education to be avoided which otherwise impair their effectiveness:

1. That people can be told *how* to develop and that 'I know and can do the telling. The learnings of development are gained through experiences. The role of the worker is to encourage and to help people to consider consequences. His own experiences should be used as guides not as directions.
2. The idea that this person has something to 'sell' to other people in terms of motivation. Motivation comes from within and his function is to help people to discover the bases for motivation, what concerns them about its direction to stimulate them to action and to support them in their determination to act for their and other's good.

This means that he is less an instructor in the sense of 'this is the way to behave' and more a person who has the skill to provide and use situations and opportunities that expedite self-learning. His own experiences are not denied the young people – how can they be if he is a warm and lively person – but they are used as a stimulant rather than a template.

If there is a central theme in the purpose of youth work it is the belief that human beings reach their deepest satisfactions through relationships and that it is in communion with others that they learn to express themselves. In order to commune one must first have become independent, freed from coercive pressures and compulsion. Youth work can be the bridge of independence and freedom for young people but it is a bridge that leads from somewhere else. How long they tarry on the bridge and how they use the time may be their decision. 'Do not rescue me prematurely' . . . 'is one part of adolescent response to adult intervention. Religious folk are vulnerable to the temptation of wanting to force the issue. They offer the Pearl of Great Price and they fear its rejection. But urgent and passionate preaching of the Gospel, at the right time and in the right place, is far removed from an over-anxiety which makes us want to burgle men's souls. Over-anxiety springs in fact, from our own inner uncertainty'.[1] But sooner or later the young have to move off

[1] *Social Group Method and Christian Education* – F. W. Milson, Chester House 1963.

the bridge if only because of the pressure of those following behind and if they move forward it is to discover that independence and freedom take on new responsibilities. During his time on the bridge he can be helped to experience the deepening of relationships, a growing confidence in relating to different groups, an awareness of self particularly as it is reflected by the group, the strength of his own resources in meeting new situations, the conflicts between groups and the techniques that can be used to accommodate differences and maintain a community of work. Added to this will be the opportunities for new experiences in many forms, some of these experiences may be in activity pursued earlier at school but with a new dimension, to discover likes and dislikes, agreements and disagreements, to exercise choice and experience the consequences. Many units of youth work see themselves as microcosms of society, workshops where young people can experience 'community', experiment within the confines of the club without 'coming to harm'. For many this is too phoney and protective and if the object is to experience community why divorce them from it in this one area of their lives?

Undoubtedly the isolating of the young into a service which offers opportunities for useful pastimes with a little 'preparation for citizenship' thrown in is no longer acceptable either as meeting the needs of the clients or society. If some young people wish to have nothing more than social clubs where they can have fun then we should accept the objective and not try to justify the work by coating the pill. However the majority of the youth work agencies will have additional purposes for providing a service and will make this known both to the workers and the clients. Naturally the purpose dictates programme. This is clearly seen in the uniformed organizations and less obviously so in the other youth groups. But, nevertheless, what is done, or perhaps more applicable what is not done, tells us something of the purpose and what needs the unit is trying to satisfy. The social and recreational needs of the young are the criteria of good youth work.

Schools and Social Education

Youth work cannot ignore the developments of social education in the Secondary Schools. The youth worker may see his work as more social than educational and there are many reasons for the misunderstanding, at times almost deliberate, of the roles of the school and the club. Social education begins in the primary stage of education and the best primary schools offer the child freedom in creativity through play, lots of scope for originality and sharing in undertakings with others, where the wise teacher allowing the child to move at its own pace knows when to intervene in the learning process and, equally important, when to hold back. Here the preparation for the 'lesson' and the tidying-up are all part of the same thing. The child feels able to move around and to a large degree is not circumscribed by dos and don'ts. The approach to the teacher is not one of subservience or fear. It is at times as equals but at others of acceptance of an authority like that of the patient, firm but understanding parent. Here there are few of the pressures which will be met in the upper classes of the junior school and the secondary school. And yet it has to do its job of 'inculcating' approaches to more educational matter. There is a great similarity between the primary stage of formal education and the primary stage of preparing for manhood and womanhood and between the roles of the primary school teacher and the youth worker. But young people come from secondary schools to the youth service and it has only been recently that official sources have seen the possibility of combining academic attainment and the meeting of social needs as a viable proposition for the secondary school. Of course educators have always talked about preparing their charges for the rigours of adult life and have made attempts to offer experiences to their pupils beyond the academic and vocational training which increasingly in a technical and meritocratic society they have been called upon to do. But the Newsom Report[1] gave expression to much common ground between the functions of secondary education and the youth service in the social education of young people. The Report suggested that the personal and social needs of the young could be met by a more realistic relationship with the adult world; extension of practice in skills and activities as well as a closer link with career and working life through time spent away from, the classroom and the inclusion in the teaching programme of

[1] *Half our Future* (Newsom Report) H.M.S.O. 1963.

adults whose experience of the world of work would be beneficial to the pupils, and areas where the pupils could exercise choice and have experience in decision-making. It further suggested extension of the school day to allow for extra-curricular activities, societies, clubs and interest groups.

To recognize this as desirable for the social development of young people is one thing, to operate it quite another. The youth worker needs to understand, not only the aspirations but the practicalities. He may want to work with others to achieve the ideals but he also has to work with the present situation. The instances of real involvement in the social education of the adolescent in line with the Newsom Report are few and too many schools remain isolated from the community despite reports and pronouncements by Ministers. A long heritage of buildings mono-purpose built, an attitude both on the part of society and the teachers that the purpose of education is academic and vocational and a suspicion that youth service activities distract from that main purpose will not be overcome quickly or necessarily by legislation. In previous Working Papers the Schools Council has already noted a growing awareness of the necessity for teachers to be conscious of the needs of individual pupils, while they are still at school, and equally of the school-leaver's expectations of life in an adult society. This latter demands a knowledge of his reactions when he takes up employment and an awareness of the social life and behaviour of the young adult. 'The successful schools are those which have decided to take the individual and not the class, as their educational unit.'[1] 'In practical terms it is extremely difficult for teachers in an over-populated school situation to pay as much attention to the needs of the individual as may be desirable . . .'[2] But 'any project aimed at the remedial use of the school supposes not merely curriculum reform or modifications in traditional methods but a recognition of the fact that school and class-room climate, ways of organization, apparent roles, prestige factors, in short the whole sociology of the school itself are involved, particularly the willingness of adolescents to stay on and con-

[1] Schools Council: Working Paper No. 11 *Society and the Young School leaver.*

[2] *The Schools and the Youth Service* N.A.Y.S.O. 1969.

tinue their education. . . . Teachers of adolescents, whoever they may be, need a profound, informed insight into the psychology of those they aspire to teach, and the mastery of educational method as well as of subject matter. All their efforts may, however, come to naught if the organization of the school implicitly contradicts what they set out to do: and if education is in conflict with the culture of the homes and streets from which the pupils come, as it so often is and may of necessity have to be, then it is of capital importance that teachers and school should have high prestige to reinforce the lessons which the warm, friendly relations make possible.'[1]

The youth worker, at the moment, may have to recognize the limitations of the school system in its role as social educator. For instance if the youth worker believes that freedom of choice, the organization and regulation of their own affairs, being able to question, challenge and disagree with authority, is part of the purpose of social education of the young he will recognize that the school organization may not be able to allow such expressions, certainly in the 'normal' curriculum. More ways of encouraging these possibilities, however, are being introduced in some schools. What the school is attempting to achieve in social education and the lengths to which it can go in allowing pupils to exercise personal responsibility and choice, the understanding of the limits to personal freedom within a society (school), experiment in new fields of activity where success or failure is not related to academic attainment and finding some sense of fulfilment through relationships with peers and adults should be taken up by the youth worker and enhanced in the youth group situation.

Youth Work and the Community

The Gulbenkian Report[2] comments that both central government and local authorities having developed a largely self-contained and coherent structure for the youth service, have in recent years become conscious of the need to relate the youth

[1] *Adolescents in School and Society*: W. D. Wall: National Foundation for Educational Research in England and Wales 1968.

[2] *Community Work and Social Change*: Celouste Gulbenkien Foundation: 1968.

service more closely to the community at large. The report goes on to give reasons for this need as due to the greater mobility of young people, wider choice in the use of leisure, earlier maturation and the demand for adult rights and privileges at an early age, greater economic independence and the falling age of marriage, the rising standard of education and the intellectual gap between the generations. It goes on to suggest that the youth worker may work more closely with other workers and agencies in the community and possibly have responsibilities which are not confined to young people. This latter has certain things to say to all who work within the youth service but appears to be more directed to the 'full-time' or professional youth worker than the 'part-time' or voluntary worker, for the latter in his vocation or other voluntary work may well be doing just this. The Youth Service Development Council in Youth and Community Work in the 70's talks a great deal about community development but with no clarity of definition or clear guidance as to how the youth service can be related to the community at large. Much of what is proposed, it would be argued, was being achieved clearly by some local organizations, themselves being evidence of community development. In fact the Report states (para 237) 'the club in future must be and must be seen to be what it has already become for a growing number of workers in the field – a base of operations in a neighbourhood rather than a segment cut out for those who want to use it'. But why should not some people have such a 'segment'? It seems reasonable, and within the principle that people need to feel free to choose and be self-directing in what they do with their own time, that some people for some of their leisure time wish to segregate themselves. As the Editorial in Youth Review (Autumn 1969) said 'Dare we also point out that the Report says very little about the possibility that at least some young adults may want relaxation and entertainment as an alternative to being "publicly active"? And cannot this be seen as part of youth service provision?'

Since the publishing of the Albemarle Report there has been an increase in the number of youth workers operating with groups of young people unfortunately called the 'unattached', meeting them on their own territory whether this be in coffee-bars, discotheques, pubs, street corners or other 'hang-outs'.

This part of youth work, it is felt by many, has not been exploited sufficiently and may still be seen as experimental and exploratory rather than essential if the youth service is to meet the special needs of youth and *all* youth and not just those who feel able to avail themselves of the *club approach*. During the 1960's there has, also, been an increase in the numberof schemes of community service attracting some young people not in youth club membership and in those two approaches we see some community needs being met in terms of attempts to reduce the alienation of some young people (the 'unattached') and through service to the community by young people. However these needs are not only met by establishing 'new' organizations or creating a new type of worker. Many youth groups, voluntary or full-time staffed, have taken into their programmes both service to the community and attempts to reach out to those not attracted to clubs. Undoubtedly they have been more successful in the former than the latter. But much of this has not been the result of a deliberate and consciously co-ordinated community appraisal of the needs of the neighbourhood or of the various agencies at work in the neighbourhood. This has resulted in waste of scarce resources of man-power as well as materials and more 'underlapping' than overlapping in meeting people's needs. Some Church Clubs for instance have seen youth clubs formed by a local church which have drawn young people from existing clubs or groups and then added nothing to the experiences they were having previously and where it might have been wiser to have made resources available to what already existed in order to enhance the work being done. Some local education authorities have failed in this respect too, by not making more resources available to an existing agency in order that it might build on good foundation, rather than 'filling the gap' by creating another unit of work. Such procedures tend to chase the same customers and fail to meet the needs, or even contact, new ones. If youth work is to be seen as part of community development the policy makers need to be aware of the danger of alienating sources of youth and community service if it ignores existing institutions. Likewise, the existing institutions, like the school and the church, must be ready to involve themselves in community and neighbourhood planning and become less insular and self-centred.

The full-time youth worker talks about his feeling of isolation and whilst there are many aspects of this, one is his uncertainty about his work in relation to work being done by other agencies in the community. This is true of the voluntary club leader who works on two or three nights a week often with no contact with others doing a similar job, except for an occasional Youth Leaders' Council when business is often too concerned with arranging functions, leagues, competitions and festivals. But this expression of isolation by youth workers has deeper implications. A concept of community development or community work is perhaps the basis from which youth work, as other social work in all its aspects, should begin rather than the present one of trying to fit youth work and other social work as pieces of a jigsaw into a picture called community. The United Nations definition of community development 'designates the utilization under one single programme of approaches and techniques which rely upon local communities as units of action and which attempt to combine outside assistance with organized local self-determination and effort, and which correspondingly seek to stimulate local initiative and leadership as the primary instrument of change . . .'[1] Community organization has been defined as work carried out by an individual or committee in the co-ordinating of the activities of various organizations in the community and concerning itself with the promotion of new organizations or systems to meet new or changing needs. If we see community development as a technique or method which can be carried through in any context and community organization as desirable for bringing together and maintaining a progressively more effective adjustment between social welfare needs within a geographical area, we can apply the former to youth work and see it as part of the latter. This would mean that both youth work, in general, would have a new meaning and the role of the youth worker, and particularly the professional worker, would be different to that of the traditional youth leader.

The notion of community development, in that its emphasis is on self-help, means that people in 'an area of social living marked

[1] *U.N. Document E/CN 5/291.* Programme of concerted action in the social field of the U.N. and specialized agencies (1954).

by some degree of social coherence'[1] are helped to express their needs and stimulated to local initiative and to produce leadership as the primary instrument of change. This requires help sometimes from external sources which may well be some person with expertise in helping people to articulate their needs and, understanding what is practicable in view of the demands on scarce resources, helping them to promote action. The decision-making and direction of the action is entirely in the hands of the people and not directed by the outside expert in the belief that the process of decision-making, consideration of actions and the achievement of some sort of welfare programme brings fulfilment to people, is their own and tends to stand the test of time. The important elements of this approach are:

1. The needs are those of the local people rather than 'assumed' needs
2. Local initiative and local leadership are essential for the 'health' of the community
3. External assistance is non-directive

Putting youth work into this community context means having a different approach in total than the present one. Such an approach would entail partnership not only of the youth work agencies in given areas but joint exploration with other educational and social work agencies where all concerned see a need to consult with groups of adults and young people, and not only those in 'organizations', to find what kind of services and resources are required or which need to be enhanced and modified in order to meet the varying needs. This requires a special kind of skill and it may well be the place for the external assistance, that is, the trained worker who sees his prime function as that of enabling people to meet, discuss, articulate and propose lines of approach. He will require skill in knowing how to explore and carry out social investigation, to analyse the community he will be serving so that he can assist the reconciling of various approaches and 'vested' interests, to help those working with groups to see their work as part of a total plan which includes a variety of units meeting special needs or offering different kinds of opportunities for the same or different individuals and that their work makes sense only in relation

[1] McIver and Page: *Society*: Macmillan & Co., Ltd. (1961).

to all the other work carried out in that community. Youth work may have been more fortunate in one respect than other educational and social work in that clubs for the most part are voluntary and have been *led* by local adults, products of the community they serve and with the same desire to initiate or take part in a programme of community development. But there has been a growth of the imported leader, both professional and non-professional, which has the tendency to move the work out of its community context by assuming that some areas, probably those which already feel alienated from the decision-making processes, are unable to do things for themselves and are not capable of producing leadership from within their own ranks. So we are back to imposing what people from one social milieu believe is *good* for others, instead of accepting that what is good is that people shall have the opportunities to exercise their rights to self-determine what they *feel* to be good for them. So often, then, we see youth work which bears little or no relationship to the immediate community – there is a great degree of 'sameness' about club work no matter what differences there are in the social and cultural environments in which the club is set.

Chapter Five

Principles

Because there can be no list of remedies for every situation the youth leader meets in his day-by-day contact with young people, no prescriptions or recipes which he can have at his finger tips to meet every exigency and because, no matter how much theoretical knowledge he has about human growth and behaviour, of society, of activity skills or group dynamics and despite his years of service, he needs some way of checking that his actions and responses are in acceptable ways and for acceptable ends.

As we have seen in Chapter One the pioneers of youth and social work functioned with a basic moral certainty founded on their deep religious convictions and a duty, moral or spiritual, based on their privileged position towards those they saw as less privileged. The rights and duties under which they worked, the way in which they worked and the ends which they strived would be seen as acceptable to that society. We live in a different society today and the role of the youth or social worker or educator is less clearly defined and, unlike the doctor, his role and ethical code is less clearly understood by society. This is as true of the professional as the lay worker. And yet is the main source of sanction from which he derives the principles which guide him in his work.

The expectations of our society in relation to a whole range of human activity are difficult to define. There is a great deal of confusion and conflict and even contradiction about these expectations and the youth leader may receive little guide or direction as to how he should act in his relations with the people he serves. He will receive advice from many sections of society much of which he will term as unhelpful and even restrictive. There will be one section of the society which should offer him guidance, namely, his agency or sponsoring body whether this be his Church, local education authority or voluntary agency. This group of people will have some reason for establishing the particular piece of work. These reasons should form the philosophy and aims and give some indication of the role of that particular youth leader. The aims should reflect the needs of the people to be served and may well be expressed in practical ways of how those needs can be met. They might be less directive and allow the worker to interpret the aims, or desired ends, according to the way the needs are expressed by the people who join the organization or avail themselves of the services offered. Both the agency and the worker must be concerned to convey the aims or purpose of the organization to the 'clients' as soon as possible. A criticism levelled at some church work is that it has appeared to offer a service to young people with 'no strings attached' and then put them in an embarrassing situation or given them a feeling of rejection when after a period of membership and a growing feeling of belonging they are expected to attend a number of church services or functions in order to maintain their membership. If the sponsoring body feels a need to make certain rules about membership then these should be communicated to the applicant at once.

The agency, organization or sponsoring body may be part of a larger community service or an isolated, insular piece of social work. Recent interest in community, stemming from intensified urbanization, social and geographical mobility, the problems of re-housing, poor physical and social environments, a feeling of alienation from areas of decision-making by so many people, suggests that the social worker needs to look at a smaller area than generalized society as his source of sanction. Furthermore it is suggesting that it is unwise, if not impossible, for agencies and workers to operate in isolation. This focus on community emphasizes the importance of recognizing the cultures and sub-cultures in our society and the implications of sub-culture on the clients who use the social services.

The youth leader who has grown up in the area may have more to offer to the young people he serves because of his understanding of the sub-cultural differences and the norms of behaviour which may be different to the generalized norms of society, and because he 'speaks the language' of the locality. Society's expectations may be desirable in terms of how young people should behave in the long run but it may tend to force the pace and alienate young people from their background.

Many leaders are aware of the conflict at home when the young person through the influence of the club begins to behave in a manner different to that expected in the home. At the other end of the scale the youth leader has to be aware of the influence of school and home where the desire may be to change the young person's behaviour from that of the norm of his locality and where the club, in appearing to support the sub-cultural norms of the locality puts undue strain on the young person. With more young people staying on at school after fifteen, more of them having home-work and the school having first claim for out of school activities the youth leader needs to be very sensitive to the effect this has on his members and on his relationships with parents and school teachers.

In one respect society gives a clear direction to the youth leader. This is to do with the law. Society's assumption is that the youth leader is law-abiding, that is, on the side of law and order and he has no special privilege in law because of his role as youth leader no matter how he feels about the confidentiality of his work. In this respect he does not have the same claims to sanction as does the doctor or parish priest. The law will treat him as another citizen within the bounds of what is lawful behaviour and, beyond this, may expect him to help young people to respect the law and understand its limitations. Some youth workers who operate outside the more orthodox setting, meet groups of young people in situations or have information about actions which are near the limits in what is lawful, and feel that in order to maintain their contacts in the hope of helping these young people they have to be allowed to decide how they shall act. They have to face the consequences of so deciding, of course, and on occasions are allowed such discretion. No matter how the agents of the law, such as the police, feel about this the general public may be less sympathetic even hostile to the worker. Of paramount importance in such situations is the attitude and support of the agency. There is an area of illegal practices in many sub-cultures from petty pilfering to larceny, from under-age drinking to drug taking, but no matter how acceptable these may be within the sub-culture, the youth leader will lose any respect he may have gained if he associates himself with these activities or gives the impression of condoning them.

Acceptance

This brings us to the first ethical concept of acceptance. Stated simply it is the recognition of the worth of the individual, regardless of his circumstances, status, religion, race, politics or behaviour and the desire to foster the growth of human dignity and self respect. It is to do with the belief in the sanctity of human life and the right of every individual to a full and satisfying experience of living. Acceptance here is not to do with the policy of taking into membership any or all applicants for membership for this may be unwise in terms of what the organization can then offer to people in relationships and real experiences. It is not to do with numbers but what one has to offer in personal terms. Although we use the term individual we need to recognize that this is somewhat de-humanizing and the leader should think in terms of persons. And persons in their wholeness and not in parts or roles as members, apprentice, choir member, inside right, captain of table tennis, and so on, The genuine educator is concerned with the person as a whole, both with the actual as he is now with all the strengths and weaknesses which stamp him as a unique person, and with his potential, what he can become.

Such an educator is aware of all the form-giving influences in a person's life, of the home, school, neighbourhood, press, radio, television, daily custom, rumour, science, music, art, play, work and that he is one element in all this. But he may be distinct in that he can be concerned with the wholeness of each individual person and involved in the way each receives messages from and is influenced by all the other form-giving elements in his life and helping him through the development of criticism and discrimination to arrive at a selection of what he believes to be right for him, which will be different to the selection made by the leader or any of his contemporaries. There will be similarities in many areas of influence but the totality will be unique to the individual person. Understanding this prevents the stereotyping of people based on previous experiences of meeting and knowing about people from similar backgrounds. There is a great temptation for all of us to type-cast people and to pre-judge them before we have had a mutual experience. The three young men who appear at the door of the club dressed in leathers, with hair reaching their shoulders, looking unsmilingly at whatever is going on are more likely to produce the thought, 'Oh dear, trouble' from a number of adults than a move which demonstrates a non-judgemental attitude. He may not approve, privately, of certain modes of dress or behaviour but he has to ask himself how his own attitudes, beliefs and values affect his demonstration of acceptance, and whether by some response, inflection of voice or facial expression he is expressing disapproval.

Acceptance is not something he can give from a superior position to an inferior. It is a real going-out to another person, it is love, that love which transcends liking or tolerance, or the different feelings about what is and what is desirable. It is easier to demonstrate acceptance to those we are attracted to than those, who for some reason, we find unlikeable. We have more time for some people than for others and we demonstrate this in our private lives in the way we choose our friends, but as youth workers we cannot allow this sort of judgement to influence our practice. Disapproval can be felt by the way other members are approved by the leader. Young people feel very keenly that some of their number receive a closer relationship and higher status because they conform to a pattern or have the attributes which are approved by the adults in the club. Responsibilities and privileges need to be carefully allocated and the tendency to use terms like 'good' member, 'loyal', 'reliable', 'faithful', to describe some in front of other members may be seen as disapproval of the latter. Perhaps the worst form of non-acceptance and possibly the most persistent in youth clubs is the ignoring of the opinions of a number of members, or by not deliberately seeking it, or where it is voiced treating it as less value than that of others.

At other times the leader's understanding and practice of acceptance will be tested in relation to behaviour which the adults and other members of the club see as undesirable. It is at these times that his initial expression of professional regard and love of human beings has to be demonstrated whilst actively disapproving of the particular piece of behaviour. As the members as individual persons experience his reactions to them in a number of different situations so they come to understand that his love for them continues even when they are called to task about some behaviour pattern. They appreciate that his annoyance or show of indignation does not mean that he withdraws his love or that he asks for anything in return for his love.

Self-determination

The youth worker will want to encourage self-help as a means to growth in self-confidence and in ability to take on more and more responsibility for one's own affairs. He will use his relationships with the individual person and groups of persons to help them become more free and self-reliant than dependent on others and the organization. The worker's respect for the individual person's right to determine his own life limits or directs his influence and guidance where he and young people are concerned with decision-making. He recognizes the ambivalence in a society which seems to offer great freedom of choice, where the young person is expected to make independent decisions with little direction or guidance and on the other hand is pressured to conform to a way of life which negates his very individuality. Some young people who come under the influence of youth workers will have developed their resources quite adequately in the area of self-determining, others will have had less opportunities to develop their own resources and instead of feeling free may feel lost.

This is, then, no easy attribute to acquire and individuals will vary considerably in their ability to cope with the consequences of a self-determining life. It is not the same as saying, 'I can do as I like with my life', for this freedom to choose carries with it heavy responsibility. Choice always involves other people. So that in 'doing what I want to do' must always pose the question of how this effects other people and does it deny in the very act the rights of others to be self-determining. Choice so often means conflict. The elementary principle of doing what I want to do ought not to interfere with the freedom of others and desire has to be tempered with morality. Freedom comes not from following the unrestraints of desire but by allowing desire to be conditioned by reason. Martin Buber in *Between Man and Man*[1] says '. . . youthful spontaneity must not be suppressed but allowed to give what it can. But then the delicate but important influence begins. The teacher brings criticism and

[1] *Between Man and Man*: Martin Buber (1947) Fontana Library.

instruction into the experience and, no matter how unsophisticated or unacademic, the young people begin to encounter ascale of values which may be quite constant however individualistic and the more unacademic and the more unindividualistic and self-discovered the more real and deep is the experience, the more there is a preliminary declaration of what alone is right and wrong the more there will be resignation or rebellion'. We misunderstand the process needed if we see it in terms of authority at one end and complete freedom at the other if each young person is to be creative, original, self-reliant and yet be helped to reach a personal set of values which will be meaningful to him. The values, beliefs and standards of the social educator are a challenge to the young person, and he allows them to be challenged. He learns to recognize when he is interfering in the learning of self-determination through the use of his authority, when he is putting tidiness, order, other people's assessment of the club, the avoidance of conflict above the needs of individual young people struggling with the consequences of making choice. His influence proceeds from his integrity. The authority the worker has derives from his sponsoring agency and it may have very definite rules or conditions governing who might be in membership of the club and what is permissible and not permissible on its premises. The agency has every right and a duty to define such limitations to the leader and in turn to the prospective clients. All social group work has its limitations and the workers and clients have to work within these and it would be an unreal learning situation if one encouraged clients to think that there were not such limitations imposed on all of us in our group affiliations in the community. But within these limitations the young people should be allowed as much freedom and decision making as possible. Some of their decision-making will test the limitations imposed and this should be seen as a very important part of tempering desire with reason.

Within the organization there will be numerous opportunities for a young person to exercise choice, in choosing with whom he will associate, in activity, in the way he responds to corporate decisions, whether he wishes to be part of the formal structure of the club and so on. He will also be involved in making choices outside the club and to do with his job, his family, his social activities and these will influence his behaviour in the club as much as the former and will be the concern of the leader depending on the depth of the relationship between them. The leader will be dealing with the reality of the total person and not with a part of him, that is, as member of the club. Genuine and significant learning stems from creativity and originality and this is more than 'being good at' pottery – or music or football, or only within those activities which make up the structured programme. It means providing the atmosphere that allows young people to experiment with ideas, to change the structure, to go beyond what might have become the accepted pattern of the meetings of the club, it means alerting them to the possibilities for participation in affairs outside the four walls of the club room and to an involvement in the community.

Club work can offer young people the opportunity of sharing with adults the organization and management of a going concern. Too often the limitations imposed on young people in managing their own affairs in their own club display a mistrust of their worth and deny the very opportunities of learning which so many adults claim to have struggled through in their own youth. Leaders, too, can be tempted to protect their members from experiences similar to ones they experienced and which were painful. This is, to a large extent, to deny a right to be self-determining. To quote Martin Buber again, he says one of our tasks in an industrial society is to be involved 'in keeping alive the pain of being an individual'. Failure to recognize this leads to the form of pseudo-self-government so prevalent in youth clubs where the young people are going through the motions of democratic processes and where their learning and activity is so circumscribed by the leader or his agency that the committee procedures and decisions are merely an acceptance of what has been decided elsewhere.

Confidentiality

'The human personality is a sacred thing; one dare not violate it nor infringe its bounds, while at the same time the greatest good is in communion with others.'[1]

As the youth worker becomes involved in a relationship based

[1] *Professional Ethics and Civic Morals*: Emick Durkheim: Routledge & Kegan Paul.

on trust he must recognize that what passes between him and the member is confidential. There is less a problem when the information is given to him with the proviso 'this is in confidence' than in the situation where he receives information in what appears to be general conversation or where he and the member are chatting about a number of issues during which the member expresses opinions about himself and others and his attitudes to institutions in society. He must always assume that personal information, no matter what the circumstance in which it is passed on, is personal, given in trust and therefore confidential unless the member gives permission for it to be used in another context. This will be so with information about the individual members no matter how much of it, the leader believes, is common to other people. Obviously there is some information not of the confidential nature which will be available to other workers in the club, such as, names, addresses, place of work or school, parents and, according to the requirements of the particular club, or part played in activities and the formal structure of the club. But whatever other records a leader keeps containing information of individual members they must be professionally guarded. The relationship between leader and member will deepen according to the way he uses the trust placed in him by the member and will be destroyed if he uses any of this information outside the relationship. This involvement in someone else's life is a privilege. The power it gives to the leader can be used to help the young person grow or misused to destroy his faith in adults playing similar roles. At times the leader will feel that the knowledge he has about an individual member suggests that other people, perhaps within another discipline such as the Youth Employment Officer, the factory Personnel Officer, the Church Minister, could offer help to this young person. No matter what the leader's relationship is with such a person and no matter how subtle he may be in soliciting their help, his ethical duty is to discuss this with the member and seek his approval before making such an approach to another adult.

Some of the confidential knowledge the leader has will be tested in situations in the club between the particular member and other members. He may see the member going through some agony because he is withholding from his contemporaries something of his private life and the leader may feel that the other members would be more sympathetic if the information was disclosed. It is not his place to disclose it and he will have to suffer the agony of this. However, his relationship should be such that he can help the member to reconsider whether it would be wiser to have the information disclosed. Whichever way the member decides must be accepted and supported by the leader. At times the leader will receive information which he feels he is unable to keep wholly confidential because the law demands he release it. Where he is in a situation like this he must make his position quite clear to the member or members. In the process of hearing information involving unlawful behaviour he must state his position at the onset and re-state his position as more information is given. He must make it clear to young people that if they wish to involve him they must accept his right and duty to decide what action he takes after receiving the information. Opportunity is afforded, then, to the young people to continue divulging information or not to proceed. The choice is theirs. The consequences should be clear. The leader makes the point that they can withhold information, although they have divulged part of the case, and what his actions will be, and if they wish to use him further he is willing to be used as long as they appreciate his position as a youth worker, confidant and citizen.

Guiding Principles

Having looked at some of the philosophical and ethical assumptions on which youth work has been built we turn our attention to a number of principles which guide our day-to-day practice. These can be reduced to three:

1. Pursuing the purpose of youth work
2. Using one's growing self-awareness
3. Starting where young people are.

The Albemarle Report quoting the Sir John Maude definition of the aims of the Youth Service (chapter 1) went on to say 'The aim of the Youth Service is not to remove tensions so as to reach towards some hypothetical condition of "adjustment" to individual or social life. It is to help towards ensuring that those tensions which are social accidents, often both fruitless and oppressive, shall not submerge the better possibilities of children during their adolescence.' There can be said to be an overall purpose for youth work in terms of offering opportunities to young people by challenging them to be creative and adventurous; to learn how to respond to different social situations; to reach forward to maturity and to see a part for them in the development of society. Social education is to do with change, to help in the move from one state to another and only by being successful in the tasks at adolescence can a young person change to the next tasks facing him as an adult. But all club situations will not be seen as concerned with change. Much of the purpose of club life is seen, or should be seen, by young people as fun. They will not put themselves in the position of being 'educated' in the narrow institutionalized meaning of that word. It is the skill of the leader which enables young people to learn and to change through the enjoyable experiences of group activity.

The youth worker needs to safeguard the individual members from the pressures of other adults who may use young people to acquire glory and status for the organization to the detriment of some members. Activities may be seen as ends in themselves rather than means so that the success the activity brings the club is a greater criteria than the learning experiences it affords the members. This is not to say that standards within activity should not reach the highest possible level but maintaining the level may rule out the participation of many members. The sponsoring agency may wish to add something of its own character to the overall purpose of youth work for it may consider the highest form of this purpose is in working for other people in the community, belonging to the Church, serving a political party and as already stated this would be communicated to the members.

Self-awareness

Self-awareness is to do with the youth worker's ability to use his personality, knowledge, understanding and skill in a consciously controlled manner. He will need to know a great deal about himself, his likes and dislikes, how much his own background prejudices him to certain people, how easily he identifies with people he assumes have had, or are having, similar experiences to his own; where his biases lie both with people and activity; what his attitude to authority is and how this has come about: what things influence him most about people. These are his strengths and weaknesses and they can work for him or against him in his relationships. The nearer he gets to accepting himself the more he will be able to accept others and in the process of trying to understand himself and why he reacts the way he does the more he will be able to understand others. This growing self-awareness will help him to a deepening insight into the similar struggles of young people. The more we struggle with understanding the self the clearer it becomes that we cannot know what is right, in an absolute sense, for others. It is through this self-awareness we learn the difference between sympathy – feeling sorry for someone – and empathy – feeling with a person and not being so emotionally caught up in the situation that we cannot offer real help.

The leader develops a sensitivity to words and actions as they affect different individuals and helps to assess this in the responses to him so that the image he has of himself is nearer that held by others. He also becomes aware of how certain actions and decisions made by some members affect the feelings of others.

Starting Where Young People Are

This sounds very obvious but so often the start is made from where the worker would like the young people to be rather than where they actually are. The position is summed up in the delightful story of the motorist, who was hopelessly lost, asking an old local in some tiny village for directions and receiving the reply 'If I was you I wouldn't start from here.' Too often starting where young people are is measured by overt behaviour, the way they dress or fail to say please and thank you, by their approach to other young people or their avoidance of adults rather than trying to assess their world view. If we cannot know all we might like to know about their previous experiences in order to understand their responses we can afford them the opportunities to express their world view – how things appear to them. It is difficult to see how a leader can offer real help on this journey through adolescence unless he starts from the individual's view-point. The leader needs to enter his world not as an equal or to be like him but in order to talk with him about his experiences. Young people do not wish us to be like them, or to act like them, for when we attempt this it is patronizing and offensive. This does not mean that we cannot enjoy some of the things they enjoy or have similar views to theirs but the young have to feel that this is genuine and that we can say why it is so rather than appearing to be 'one of them' or on their side. At the same time we may not accept some of the things they do but we have to accept that this is lawful to them at this stage of their development. They may not want to remain in this state long and we may be instrumental in helping them to change. Care has to be taken not to under-value or over-estimate their desire and ability to cope with change.

Young people will vary in their starting points and the degree to which they can accept the challenge to change. Perhaps we under-estimate their ability to face new situations but there is little point in throwing them in at the deep end when the same results can be learned step by step. Some of the unsophisticated and non-verbal means of communication displayed by young people in horse-play, physical contact, quick-fire emotional outbursts demonstrate where they are and although the natural feeling on the part of the leader is a wish that they did not behave this way, he needs to remind himself that this is where these young people are in the process of growing-up. His concern is how do I help. He needs to be aware that this is the form of communication they know and which is meaningful to them and that they may not, as yet, have learned other forms of communicating.

Other young people, possibly in the same club, may have reached a different point in the growth process and require releasing from the norm. They may need to be helped to move away from the club in order to continue to grow and the leader has to take care that he does not manipulate the situation to retain the services of a 'good' member. Care must be taken not to rationalize by suggesting such a person gives back something to the club by remaining as a helper when in the best interests of that person he would be better served by moving away from the club.

Chapter Six

WORKING WITH GROUPS

The primary function of youth leadership is that of helping or enabling young people through their group affiliation to a 'better' understanding of self and of becoming a more integrated, satisfying and effective person. A worker in this role is concerned with the organization of groups and how to provide the greatest satisfaction for the members. This entails skill in understanding what people are seeking from such experiences of group affiliation and how he can help individuals and groups through their activities whilst in membership to discover opportunities for enjoyment and growth. Members bring to the group their total life experience and this means experiences of their other group affiliations, for everyone in the present complex society is a member of different types of social groups. The values, norms, standards, status and feeling of worth they experience in other group situations will be brought to a new group experience along with their expectations or goals or desires they see the new group meeting. A knowledge of the individual's other-group experiences and an understanding of the nature and function of groups, is therefore, desirable if the youth worker is to approach his task scientifically. 'Human beings can be understood only in relation to other human beings. What a man is, is reflected by the behaviour of other men towards him. What a man thinks of himself is his judgement of the reactions of other men to him. The behaviour of any individual is a mirror of his total life-experience, most of which is in groups. If one is to understand an individual, one must know the groups to which he belongs. Every individual has a different status in each of the variety of groups to which he belongs. The same individual will exhibit different patterns of behaviour in different groups.'[1]

The groups to which a person belongs can be divided into

[1] *Social Group Work Practice*: Wilson and Ryland: Houghton Mifflin Co. 1949.

two main categories: primary, that is where the members of the group have a high degree of interdependence and a regular face-to-face relationship, such as the family, friendship groups, work-units, clubs, classes in school or church, immediate neighbourhood, and secondary groups which might be seen as the Church, the factory, a political party, the community made up of many primary groups. Krech, Crutchfield and Ballachey[1] use the terms psychological groups and social organization to distinguish between those small intimate groups where each member's behaviour influences the behaviour of each of the others and the beliefs, values and norms regulate mutual conduct and the integration of many inter-related psychological groups, because they are functionally related, for some stated objective. The Church can be seen as a social organization within this definition, the more so since it has extended its function to cater increasingly for social as well as religious needs both for those in membership of the Church and for other groups of people who may not be in, or desirous of, membership of the Church. The largest units of youth work may be seen as having a number of small primary groups within the larger secondary group called 'the club'. Some of the groups to which a person belongs may be seen as 'natural groups'[2] where the individual has no choice (at least in the early part of his life) such as, the family, neighbourhood, school and later he may be forced to join certain groups such as the armed forces, a union, or, through lack of opportunities or real choice, a certain type of employment and place of work. Naturally, he may choose to belong to a certain neighbourhood, work in a particular factory, join the forces, a union, and the manner of joining a group, whether imposed or selected will affect his behaviour in the group. No single group will satisfy all his needs, goals, or ambitions and he, therefore, looks around for a number of groups which he believes will meet, or afford him the opportunity of meeting, more of his needs or wants.

[1] *Individual in Society:* Krech, Crutchfield and Ballachey: McGraw Hill Boots Co. 1962.

[2] *Human Groups*: W. J. H. Sprott: Pelican 1958.

Different members – different wants

The group serves different purposes for each member even when it is a small, intimate friendship group and the apparent or stated wants expressed by members may not be the real wants and this affects not only the function of the group as a whole but the individual's behaviour, both in the small group and within the organization. Those club leaders who have asked new members why they wish to join are seldom given the real reasons by the applicant even if he were able to express them in words. Perhaps the most powerful want which motivates the joining feeling is that of acceptance, wanting to belong to something bigger than one's self and to feel that others accept him as significant. This acceptance may be of him as a person either in 'general' or through some specific activity which he wishes to pursue with others. It is through this that he gains a measure of self-worth and it may be that he feels unable to get this in other group settings like home, work, or school or that he desires to gain another aspect of self-worth in a social sense which he feels unable to gain through the roles he plays in the home, at school or work. Friendship groups in the early teens serve this purpose. The group may remain fairly egalitarian for a considerable time but it is likely to have within its informal structure some form of leadership. This may be differential in that any of the members may take on leadership according to the particular task in hand, but there may well be a more dominant member whose power want is served by maintaining the group as a unit. In this case it can be said that the group meets the power want of one, or some, of its members as well as the belongingness of all of them. But as the group exists so new wants develop and this may mean the group shows signs of breaking-up. This is particularly so with the adolescent as he moves into his middle-teens and is 'pushed-along' in the youth club situation where new experiences both in the form of activities, other young people and the influence of formal leadership give him opportunities to meet his new wants. The dominant members in the small friendship group may attempt to maintain the group by extending the range of its activities, doing all things together or not at all. The youth worker needs to be mindful of this process for there is a tendency on the part of individuals to defend their group 'right or wrong' and any attempt to wean an individual away from his group may breed hostility and a closing of the ranks. This can also apply to the youth leader and his organization not able to face up to the consequences of multiple-group affiliation of the members and trying to make 'the club' sufficient for all the needs of the members. Here lies the danger of demanding loyalty.

The Formal System and the Informal System

Homans[1] hypothesized that 'if the interactions between the members of a group are frequent in the external system, sentiments of liking will grow up between them, and these sentiments will lead in turn to further interactions over and above the interaction of the external system'. If we see 'external' system as the formal structure, that is the *raison d'être* of the organization, its objects and methods of carrying out its work with the accompanying norms of conduct, the 'internal' system can be seen as the informal structure operating within the small groups. All these small groups, whether friendship or activity groups, will have an informal structure which will be peculiar to the group and such a structure will be the more important to the individuals in the group according to how often they meet together in the club situation and outside it: the similarity of their wants, status, prestige: how they are seen by the organization, usually through the youth leader's attitudes towards them as a group. Through the internal or informal system certain norms of conduct will be formed which will include expected types of response to the formal system. The more 'favourable' the small group is seen through the formal system the more likely it is that its norms of conduct will be similar to those set by the formal structure, and the less favourable it is seen, or if it feels it has lower status and prestige, the more likely it is to be at odds with the norms of conduct laid down through the formal system. Applying this to the individuals in the group, the greater the status of the person in his group the more clearly will he conform to the norms of his group and vice-versa.

In the youth club situation we have many groupings, mostly of the friendship or 'clique' type although the members may join activity-groups, not as a friendship group, but as individuals

[1] *The Human Group* – G. C. Homans: Routledge & Kegan Paul 1951.

wanting to enjoy some pastime where they have a skill or are desirous of obtaining or developing that skill. Some young people will be able to do this with little conflict in their friendship group, others will experience a great deal of conflict according to their status in the friendship group. Communication between the small friendship groups and the large total group through the formal structure may be difficult to establish and maintain. If one looks at the majority of youth clubs operating a formal members' committee it is likely that the smaller groups of highly conforming young people will be well represented whilst those who belong to groups with little status are not so. Part of this is caused by the tight control of dominant members of the low-status groups to fight off the possibility of losing members to another group as well as the desire to remain 'free' of the formal system. It may be, also, a fear of the loss of prestige, high in the small group or 'clique' but not so in the more formal, conforming group. The task of the youth worker is to understand these informal groups and to demonstrate that the organization functions best when it is, first of all, working with them and then harmonizing them with the formal structure of the organization. It is not a question of either an informal or formal system, it is both, and the autonomous nature of the small group should be preserved and seen as having special wants, and the role of the formal structure to co-ordinate these, and that the ensuing conflict and ultimate decision-making is what determines how the organization should function.

Positive Group Experiences

People join groups for a purpose. The wants which motivate an individual to seek membership of a particular group may be many and diverse. Some may be expressed or avowed, others may be unavowed. An organization like a youth club will have been established to meet certain generalized wants of young people. It will, therefore, have certain goals, some of them common to all youth groups and others more specific according to the sponsoring agency's philosophy. Each small group, whether friendship or activity group, within the organization will have goals which are acceptable to all the members of the particular small group. But neither the small primary groups or the organization as a secondary group as such, with their more generalized goals, will necessarily satisfy all the wants of all the members. However, the individual will work towards a group goal if he feels that the achievement of such a goal satisfies his personal wants. Where members experience participation in the setting of group goals there will be a higher degree of acceptance of them, for through this process the individual is likely to see the relevance of the group goals: commit himself to a decision because he has been involved in decision-making: realize that some of his wants cannot be met by the group. An important factor in this process is his perception of the role of the club leader, and through him, the sponsoring agency. The more he sees 'management' able and willing to accept change in the way goals are achieved, the better the conditions for group activity, the higher the competence of the workers both in activity skill and in their support of groups and individuals, the more he will accept the standards and the goals of the organization.

Cohesiveness and Group Culture

As already stated the average youth club in Britain consists of many small groups, often referred to as sub-groups, and the larger group or total membership. Perhaps it is unfortunate to use the term sub-groups if it implies that the large group came into being first and subsequently split up into smaller groups. Generally the members will have 'formed' groups before joining the organization or, at least, will identify with a number of friends or acquaintances who also happen to be members of the club. In any case almost from the start the members will choose to associate with a smaller number more often than with the total membership, although there will be a number of 'isolated' members.

The 'over-all attractiveness of a group to the members'[1] is termed cohesiveness and this is evidenced in the small friendship group. Activity groups may, also, have a high degree of cohesiveness but the youth leader will desire, and work towards, an experience of cohesiveness of the total membership not to replace that of the smaller groups but in addition to it. It will be through the cohesiveness of the small groups with its 'control'

[1] *Individual in Society*: Krech Crutchfield and Ballachey: McGraw Hill 1962.

of the individual members that he works in order to achieve cohesiveness of the larger group. This can be restrictive or liberal according to the motivations of the club leader and his sponsoring body. Every group with some degree of permanence will develop a group ideology of common beliefs, norms and values, and whilst these may come about through the common wants of the members and the common method of meeting them, the individual may feel unable to express his own set of beliefs, norms and values gained through other group experiences. Clubs, by their very nature, have a changing membership and the permanence of groups is short-lived requiring an approach which allows succeeding generations of members the experiences of establishing values and norms, through the formation of smaller groups and the integration of these into a larger, cohesive group. There is always the danger of establishing a code of behaviour which inhibits change and pre-disposes new members' actions and interactions. The desirable process of cohesiveness which engenders the 'we' feeling and gives satisfaction to the feeling of belonging to a group can also close the doors to new beliefs or change. Obviously members of the group may resist others joining for a number of reasons, most or all of the reasons being connected with the threat of change, structure, status and prestige of members in the group. The group may appear to be well-balanced, highly structured and giving satisfaction to its members, but it may be 'stuck', making no progress in social education terms and having developed a belief that the group is more important than the individual members.

Leadership

Leadership here, in terms of groups within the organization, must be distinguished from the position of the adult appointed as leader to the club or organization. The former is a role performed by members of the club or organization: the club leader may not be a leader in social group work terms whilst performing his task as Head of the organization.

In any group one or more members will be more dominant than the others. This dominance will be according to their influence on fellow-members, their activity in proposing, planning and carrying through what the group might do, their status in other situations and so on. The small friendship groups may be fairly egalitarian and the observer may find it difficult to name an overall leader. Part of this is because the small friendship group indulges in a wide range of activity requiring different forms of leadership and so leadership may be fairly evenly shared. In the bigger group or organization it becomes stable, a structure emerges which formalizes the positions of the members, and so we get leaders, lieutenants and followers. The youth worker and his co-workers exercise their skill with both small (primary) groups and the organization (secondary group) and accept that all members have leadership potential, certainly in the area of influencing the activities of the group. However, in all groups some members will vest more leadership in a few individuals. At the same time there will be a number of members wishing to acquire leadership to satisfy their power-drive or to benefit from the 'perks' which any organization seems to offer to those at the top of the hierarchy.

The functions of leadership are complex and vary according to the nature of the group. A number of the functions of leadership observed in adolescent groups are:

1. *Model:* or symbol through behaviour, attitudes towards other groups and authority, style of dress, presentation of self which denotes the group's ideology.
2. *Decider:* he co-ordinates the wants and activities of the group and decides what action should be taken; whether 'we' will go along with this idea or not; by and large he is given the power of final decision when there is conflict in the group.
3. *Representative:* the role of representing the group in external situations, of putting the group's point of view, receiving communications from other sources, the group's spokesman.
4. *Controller:* this is the power of giving rewards and punishment within the group. In some cases it will be severe to the extent of physical damage and expulsion, in others the withholding or giving of some small benefit.
5. *Expert:* having skills which the group needs or which give the group members reflected high status because the leader has a number of skills.

These functions can be observed in most adolescent groups with some degree of stability and apply equally to the leadership of the conforming or non-conforming group, social or anti-social group. There are not different leadership functions according to the social acceptance or non-acceptance of the activities of the group. The directions of the group's activities may be seen as undesirable but the functions of leadership can only be seen in terms of how they satisfy the group's activities.

Understanding Group Structure

The youth leader needs methods which help him to understand the nature of the natural groupings within the larger group. These groups tend to be mobile and the individual members join with other members to form 'ad-hoc' groups and join others to pursue some activity which may not attract other members of his natural or primary group. The size of the groupings will vary from couples, trios to quite large groups and undoubtedly there will be a number of isolates or members who can be observed to be on the fringe of a particular group. The sociometric method is one way of obtaining a measure of group structure and it can be used to show the inter-personal relationships between the total group as well as the strength of influence held by a number of members.

Figure II shows a number of friendship groups in a club with one member (Z) isolated except for a rather tenuous relationship with the large group (A,B,C,D,E,F,G), of seventeen to eighteen year old males who had carried their school association on into their mid-teens. They were all members of the club football team, popular with the majority of members and highly conforming in terms of the club goals. The member marked Z was to be observed with this group more often than with other groups but when the group planned activity for time outside club time he was not included. Occasionally by sheer persistence, 'hanging-on', he would be taken along by the group but if he was not present it appeared that the group were either thankful or did not notice his absence. This did not happen to any other member of the group. If one of them was occupied elsewhere in the club the group felt a need to find him and get his reactions to what was being planned. P and Q, two girls aged eighteen, were almost inseparable and it was observed that Q never came to the club alone. On the occasions that P came to the club

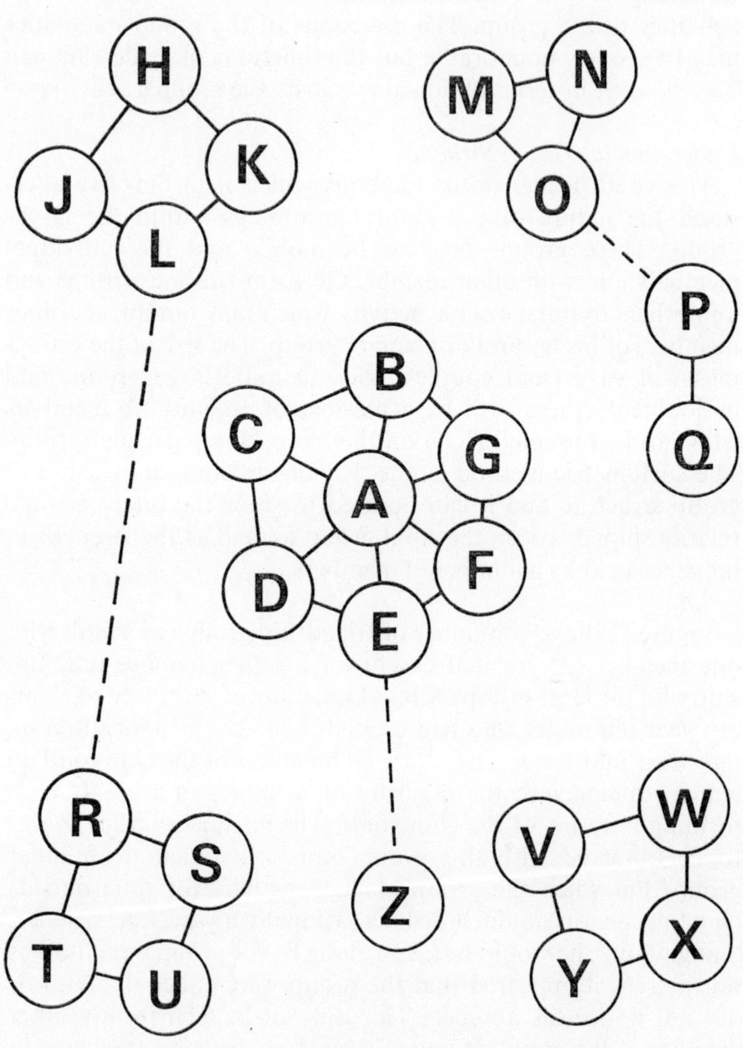

Figure II

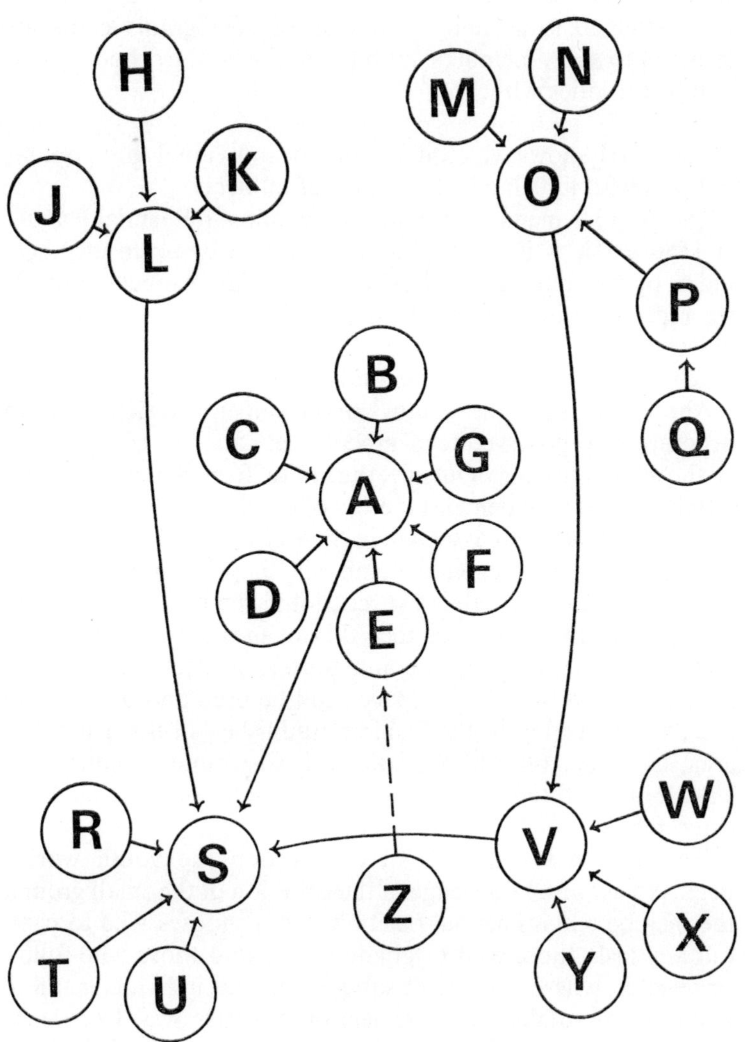

Figure III

alone she associated with three other girls M, N & O who appeared to be quite content to include her in the group. Naturally the members of all these groups associated with other members for various reasons and a number of sociograms could be designed to show members' mobility and who they choose to do certain activities with.

Figure III shows which individual or individuals are popular and powerful in being in a position of influence.

The popular member may not be the most influential person. In Figure III, A is shown as being chosen by seven members and S by five but the 'leaders' or influential members L and V are representatives of small groups, therefore S's influence is wider than that of A. In fact A chooses S for certain traits which he sees essential for the total group.

Another method the youth worker can use to define group structure is to observe the members' occupation of certain areas in the club building. Outside the more formal pursuit of an activity which may demand the use of certain parts of the building members seem to associate in 'favourite' areas. Observation of members as they enter the club will show them moving to a particular area where they expect to find the other members of their group. In some cases they do not move from these areas and give the appearance of commandeering space. There grows an expectation of how the space shall be used and other members, not behaving in the fashion established in this particular area, are fended off. This is particularly so around the coffee-bar, T.V. lounge, 'disco' areas and with the older or more sophisticated members.

Through these methods of observation the youth worker begins to acquire knowledge of the cohesion of the small groups, the members in influential positions, who chooses who to carry out any task, those who originate action and those who follow or reject it, where to contact sub-groups and individuals. He is in a position to observe movement of members away from small groups, from one sphere of influence to another, and the loneliness of some individuals rejected by their fellows as well as the aspirations of those who seek more power. He is using this observation to increase his knowledge of the wants and satisfactions of the individual members in both the formal and informal activity of the club. Within the large group, the club as a whole, the youth worker will be aware of a hierachy of status.

At the top of the hierarchy will be those members who have high status in terms of conformity to the organization's goals and code of behaviour translated in terms of positive attitudes to activities, work for the organization and general helpfulness. Their relationships with members of the staff are likely to be friendly with a fair degree of tolerance to any deviant behaviour. They will be members who have little to lose in terms of status and can take risks within the organization. Side-benefits will accrue to them because of their strong position. These may be in terms of special privileges which the staff believe to be rewards for their service to the organization and such benefits further strengthen their status. Close to this small number of members at the top of the hierarchy will be another group of members who have been given fairly high status but who may not be so secure as those at the top and feel that they have a lot to lose if they take certain risks. Whilst the group with high status may risk challenging the organization's goals and methods of achieving these the second group slightly lower in the hierarchy, may wish to do so but be afraid of losing the status they have if they are seen to be 'against the government'. At the other end of the scale there is likely to be a group with low status in the terms expressed above. In a similar way to those at the top of the scale they may feel they have little to lose and remain 'troublesome' to the organization because they are continually challenging its code of behaviour and methods of achieving its goals. Between these two groups at the top and bottom of the scale is the bulk of the membership, some aspiring to high status, some attracted to the group with low status and others who appear to have no ambition in either direction. Staff-member contact time may be disporportionate in that more time is devoted to those at the top and bottom of the scale than to the majority of members. Where there is conflict between the groups with high status and low status there is a tendency to try to resolve this by using the group at the top of the scale as the example of what the organization is attempting to achieve. This can mean the setting of certain standards or mode of conduct which suggests that some young people are not 'fit' for membership of the organization and may be a denial of the principle of starting where young people are. It also suggests that certain groups cannot be helped in terms of social development.

The Function of the Youth Worker

At the beginning of this chapter the primary function of the youth leader was defined as helping or enabling young people, through their group affiliation, to a better understanding of self and of becoming a more integrated, satisfying and effective person. This has to be put in some context like community or society or 'way of life' expressed by the sponsoring body as the Christian or democratic way of life. Lifton[1] says 'The salvation of the democratic way of life depends basically on our skill in teaching people how to use the group process as a means to preserve an environment not only where all may live, but also where individual difference is valued and where each person's happiness is truly believed to be the vital concern of all'. Perhaps the most important change in the function of the youth leader over the past two decades is reflected in the emphasis put on the skill he needs in the use of programme rather than in developing skills in activities. In the past the concern in youth work was in the occupation of young people through activities and the idea of a balanced programme tended to suggest that their needs could be met by inducing or coercing them to take part in activities which catered at separate times for the physical, intellectual and spiritual parts of a person. This ignored, or saw as of secondary importance, the preoccupation of individuals, the inter-play in social relationships which demonstrated the feelings of frustration, hostility, self-worth and of aspirations, struggles for acceptance, the difference in values, standards and expectations between the members of the same group. It failed to see that a common group activity was a different experience for each member, further, it suggested the common experience should produce the same result for each person. We are now beginning to accept that the inter-play in social relationships means as much if not more than the programme. The programme of activities is important and the more so when it grows out of the expressed needs of the members, for young people experience satisfactions from group activity whether short or long-term, and from gaining skills in performance in

[1] *Working with Groups*: W. M. Lifton: Wiley.

physical, social and artistic activities. But the youth leader as a group worker is also concerned with helping members to use the group experience or group process as expressed in the quotation above.

The youth leader is employed by a leisure-time agency, that is, an agency which accepts that young people come to it voluntarily in their free time to associate with one another for a whole range of reasons. 'If the (youth) leader is using the group-work approach he will be aware that such agency objectives, while they may serve to give general direction to his effort, must be administered in such a way as to leave individuals freedom to choose to participate in them. A group worker is neither a propagandist nor a manipulator. He interprets and makes available the resources of the agency including its outlook on life as expressed in agency objectives. Because his first concern is always the opportunity for self-directed growth, he does not coerce people to accept points of view or teach them indirectly to become subservient to leadership. Free and understanding acceptance of new values and the participation in new learning provide the essential nourishment to growth'.[1] All that goes on in the club is programme and not only those activities which can be labelled (table-tennis, football, dancing, drama, etc.). The group worker is conscious of the relationships being made in the totality of club time and whilst it may seem easier to apply group work skill to the more formalized activity group, in terms of activity performance and discussion of aims, method, responsibilities and individuals' feelings about the group activity, he must also exercise his skill with the small friendship groups and the secondary group as a whole. In fact he must always be helping the sub-groups to make their experience of the group process relevant to the larger group.

Such a worker will also be aware of the relation of the pursuits undertaken in the club to the individual members' total life in the community. In this way he understands how the individual sees the group and its activities, how he is able to use them and the relationships in the group. In this way he helps the individual to a greater awareness of self and to begin to see that the group is made up of individuals with varying

[1] *Group Work with American Youth*: G. L. Coyle: Harper & Row 1948 Chapter 11.

degrees of preoccupation or desires and that activity and relationships are being seen and used differently by individuals in his group. With sensitivity based on his knowledge of individuals the group worker helps the member to come to terms with how he stands within the group.

An example of a youth worker using this skill can be illustrated by a summary of several months' recordings of a youth club's football team.[1]

At the beginning of the football season which coincided with the re-opening of the Youth Centre after a summer recess the youth worker informed the football group he expected them to meet each Wednesday evening to discuss team selection and the previous game. He offered the group the use of his office, which was quite large, for these weekly meetings. Before the first meeting he noted down a few observations of the community from which the members were drawn and in which his agency was set. These included the facts that the large housing estate, made up of families from other mining communities throughout the country, had a reputation for 'toughness'; that the people of the small mining town and the newcomers were still two communities and in conflict and that there was a high degree of physical violence on the estate, a resolving of conflict by physical attack. He was aware of the members' inability to express feelings other than in emotional terms or through physical action. Football, and the associated betting on the pools, was almost a religion to adults and young people on the estate. Becoming a professional footballer was seen to carry very high status. Most of the male members of the club worked at the colliery.

To the youth worker the football games he had witnessed resembled tribal battles rather than games of skill. Kicking and punching opponents had been frequent both on and off the field of play. These had led to strong disciplinary action by referees and the Football Association, always seen as unjust by his members, and expressed as prejudice because they belonged to the Hillmore Estate. There was even violent behaviour between team-mates when things were not going as they hoped during a

[1] This illustration formed the basis of an article by the author published in *Youth Review* in Autumn 1968 titled 'Skill in the use of the programme'.

game. A member leaving the field of play quite voluntarily was not unusual.

The group consisted of fifteen members, one of whom had no aspirations as a player and was dubbed 'the coach' by the rest. Thirteen, including, 'the coach' were a fairly tightly knit group in the Youth Centre and on the estate. Of the other two, one was a hanger-on who came from the estate, worked at the colliery, but had little football skill. The last member of the group came from the 'old' town and worked at the colliery as a trainee having day-release to attend Technical College in a larger town some nine miles away, and was a good footballer. He was also a member of other small groups in the Youth Centre, both activity and social and fairly secure in his relationships. Whereas the other members of the football group dressed alike in jeans, open-necked blouses, and high boots, this member wore a suit or blazer and flannels.

At the first meeting the captain, appointed outside the group meeting, occupied the youth leader's chair, two other members sat on the desk and the remainder draped themselves over chairs brought in for the meeting. The youth worker sat in one of these chairs but not directly opposite the captain. At first there was a great deal of banter and the two on the table were dislodged by the captain who gradually shouted down the rest and asked 'What about last week's game, then?' Members made comments in short generalized statements like 'we was robbed', 'that ref. has always had it in for us . . .', '. . . we should have had a stack of goals . . .', '. . . they played over age players . . .', '. . . the centre-forward asked for what he got . . .' and so on. When they were unable to find other comments to make, some horseplay was indulged in between two members which brought comments from others to the effect that they should get on with the business. This led to team selection. The next two meetings followed a similar pattern with few questions directed at the youth worker. At the fourth meeting the captain asked the youth worker if he had anything to say about the team's performance. He was prepared for such a question and selecting one incident from the game gave a factual account of how he saw it build up. Some of the players could not remember the incident but those directly involved identified themselves and, in answer to the worker's questions, said what they thought about it in football terms. He asked them what their feelings were at the time. They expressed hostility and disappointment and made scathing remarks about each other's inability to react favourably, still in football terms. This brought other members of the group into the discussion in defence of, or to attack, players involved in the incident. This type of incident, repeated in subsequent weeks, reinforced the worker's observations of who influenced who in the group, of the polarizing of sub-groups even in this fairly closely knit group and of the insecurity of the 'hanger-on' who was afraid to commit himself and of the security of the odd member of the group who played an ameliorating role but was not thanked for doing so although the worker suspected the others in the group had respect for him. Later the worker suggested that each member of the group bring one incident from the next game to the subsequent group meeting. As the weeks passed the group began to talk about their feelings, the assumptions made about colleagues' ability to anticipate moves, to see the different interpretations of the same incident, to express their resentment of being 'shouted at' by members of their own team or at the decisions of the referee which they took as personal attacks. They began to challenge each other not only in football terms but related behaviour on the field to their behaviour in other situations. Gradually a form to the meetings began to develop and eventually the trainee-miner was induced to take the chair when the group was discussing incidents from the previous game. The youth worker had suggested they use the blackboard to show the positions of the players during any incident and it was at this stage that the captain suggested that the trainee-miner take over 'because he's better at doing things on the blackboard'. This may have been a genuine reason but it could also have been both a recognition of the worth of this member and face-saving for the captain who was unable to remain uninvolved in the arguments. This part of the meeting was followed by 'comments from the leader' when the youth worker helped the members to see their behaviour in terms of wants, frustration, hostility, aggression and to explain why we feel aggressive when we are frustrated. Then followed team selection, chaired by the captain and, eventually, a further item to do with arrangements for the match. The latter was quite an achievement for at the beginning of the season the group had expected the club leader 'or someone' to make all the arrangements for their game of football. As the members began to face up to criticism of each other as players in the football team they also faced up to comments about their general attitudes and behaviour in other situations, reluctantly and aggressively for some time, but as the weeks went by with less aggression although they found it difficult not to see themselves under personal attack. But this slight progress affected the whole group structure and conduct of meetings. Gradually some form to the meetings took shape, there was much more order than at the first meetings and more people were 'allowed' to take the lead for parts of the meeting.

This youth worker had set out to use the group process to help a number of young people to achieve new ways of expressing themselves, to widen their experiences of personal relationships and to gain greater satisfaction from their pastime. The other adults working in the Youth Centre had suggested that the club should not enter a football team in the Youth League in view of the behaviour of these members in past seasons. He was aware that there was much aggressiveness and show of toughness in the Centre observed in the way members handled furniture and equipment, the horseplay between members and in attitudes towards any form of authority. The football group with two exceptions, was very much a neighbourhood gang, led by Tazzer who had quite a reputation for knowing how to look after himself. He would be, automatically, captain of the team and the youth worker knew that there was no point at the beginning of the season suggesting democratic election. It was unquestionable that anyone else could be captain. Tazzer assumed the role of captain of the football team because the majority of the group had 'elected' him leader of their gang. He was also aware that the gang had difficulty in seeing a different role for itself when it was a football team and, in a way, they saw games as a legitimate form of violence and a way of flouting authority. The process of moving this group from a neighbourhood gang with its informal processes of electing a leader based on criteria which they perceived as common amongst the various groups in the community to a more formal structure where leadership needed to be based on a different set of criteria would be both slow and painful. In the way he approached and worked with the group he had to demonstrate his understanding of where they were in terms of social maturity and his interest in their activity. Interference with the conduct of their early meetings would have drawn greater hostility through their anti-authority feelings, and to the majority of the group any adult was seen as authority and a limit to their freedom. With a great deal of patience and at times questioning whether any progress was being made at all he attended faithfully the regular Wednesday evening meetings, sitting through the chaos and at times abuse directed at adults in leadership positions without being drawn to defend authority or to pronounce on the need for other values and standards of behaviour. He used the opportunities, when they were offered by the gang leader, to suggest how the group might look at their activity, timing of such contributions being most important. He also took the opportunities to have a brief word with the gang leader after the meeting, commenting on progress and encouraging him in his conduct of the meeting. This led to reciprocal treatment by Tazzer who felt no loss of status when he invited the youth worker to comment in the group meeting with the words 'You got anything to say, Chief?'

The position of John, the trainee miner, and Mick, 'the hanger-on', changed slightly over months but the gang was still suspicious and somewhat resentful of John's middle-class image. He was called a 'gaffer's-man' in early meetings and his attendance at the Technical College was referred to as 'being still at school'. He was able to take these attacks and to demonstrate affection for Tazzer and his gang. When discussion caused the gang to polarize around Tazzer and two other members, John did not take sides and his attempts to resolve the conflict eventually earned some respect and he was given a leading role. This was the group's first demonstration of learning something of the democratic process. Mick remained a hanger-on, used by the group for menial tasks which he was quite happy to perform for the reward of belonging to the group. The youth worker was not happy about this but his attempts to induce different treatment of Mick were thwarted by him as much as by the group.

It was only after these achievements that the group began to take interest in the overall organization of the football activity. Up to this stage most of the routine tasks, such as corresponding with other teams, referees, the Youth League, arranging for the laundering of strip and after match refreshments, had been carried out by the youth worker. This arose when Tazzer, who may have felt threatened by John and two other members who had challenged his authority, suggested that these jobs be farmed out to various members of the group. In this way he was still able to retain his leadership of the group and the captaincy of the team, as he said 'being captain of this lot is enough without having another job'. The final task of the youth worker was to help the group to see their position in relation to other groups in the Centre and to the total group. Getting this sort of group to experience a community of groups with sectional interests needing to co-operate and co-ordinate their demands is a difficult task. They need to be weaned slowly into acceptance of limitations which may need to be imposed for the benefit of the total membership. The practice of taking what you want for yourself with little or no thought of how this might deprive others was common in their neighbourhood. Added to this was an inability to delay rewards for greater rewards later on which they saw as a trick of adults not to concede to their immediate demands. These young people, and many adults too, on the estate, had little time-concept. To have to think about and plan for something weeks ahead of time seemed beyond their capacity. For instance, housewives on the estate, having got into debt with the shopkeepers in the old town, bought from mobile shops whose charges were much higher than the shopkeepers for the same goods. They had to pay cash to the mobile shop and seemed unable either to see that the extra they were paying would reduce their debts at the shops if they returned to them, or felt unable to strike a bargain with the shopkeepers to pay off their debt week by week as they continued to pay cash for what they now required.

Such a group may experience difficulty in understanding the agency's generalized objectives and the club leader's interpretation of these. For instance this group could not equate the worker's expression that he hoped they would win an important cup game with his veto on their selecting two players from the neighbourhood who were not members of the Youth Centre. He suspected that the injuries suffered by two of the regulars were excuses for Tazzer to bring in two better players for this game, for they made a remarkable recovery between Wednesday and Saturday when the worker pointed out the Club ruling stating that a person had to be in membership for a full week before playing in a club game. The gang in the group had no thought for two of their number who seldom played in the team, or the other members of the club, several of whom could have been approached. Reaching some form of self-government in this group and in line with the total self-government of the club was a slow process, but gradually they began to accept the higher authority of the club and apply it in their own group.

Self-government

An inevitable part of the group process is that the members will become responsible for their own affairs, exercise control and handle authority. We believe that real growth and healthy development comes from within because a person feels greater satisfaction with conclusions he reaches by his own efforts, through his own reasoning than with those forced upon him or when he feels he has been coerced into a conclusion, even when his own efforts and the conclusions may bring him pain. The more he is encouraged to use his innate capacity for decision-making and can feel some personal success in having made a decision, the more the capacity will grow and the readier he will be to make decisions in bigger issues. The worker will be aware of his influence and the support he gives the individual during this growth. He will also be conscious of the fact that this association or relationship will end and he will want to feel that the member's ability to be self-determining will depend less and less on his influence and support. In order for this growth to take place the young person must be free – free from ridicule, condemnation and persuasion, free to make mistakes as well as wise decisions and to begin to understand how and why such conclusions are wise or unwise. In youth club work the traditional vehicle for such learning is the Members' Committee, but it is doubtful whether the average Members' Committee is anything more than an activity for teaching committee procedures to a limited number of members. One can justify teaching such procedures but the process by which people become members of such a committee and the claims that it is representative and responsible are suspect. It may have no relationship to group process as we have looked at it in this chapter, in that, it is neither a natural part of the group process, nor related to real life situations experienced by young people.

Davies and Gibson[1] suggest that 'Young people's development towards maturity for their own society is in fact restricted in many cases by the members' committee, since it is a form of self-government which bears no resemblance at all to the media of democracy which young people already know best and are most likely to use outside the youth organizations.' Quoting as follows from a not untypical constitution of a members' committee one can see (a) the limited aims and the lack of relationship with, or relevance to, the group process, and (b) the restrictions in terms of control, effecting change, self-determination. '(1) One of the aims of having a members' committee is that it should be the means of training members in the techniques of committee procedure. (2) The number on the committee will be twelve with a minimum of boys or girls of three. (5) The members' committee does not have any powers to make decisions to affect the management of the club . . . it can, however, recommend and make suggestions to the management committee. (7) The members' committee cannot meet without a Leader being present and all meetings will be convened by the Leader of the Club . . .'

So *one* of the aims is training in the techniques of committee procedure, but no other aims are stated. As said above it may be laudable to acquaint people with committee procedures, learn the language and rules, practise the conducting of meetings but this is an activity or study, not necessarily self-government in practice. It could, of course, be argued that this is a voluntary activity and one need not go through a process of election to arrive at a number of participants any more than one would for table tennis, drama or discussion groups. Other statements in the constitution show how restricted the learning of self-government is in this activity by denying the young people the right to convene their own meetings, meet on their own or to make decisions about the management of the club.

[1] *The Social Education of the Adolescent*: Davies & Gibson: U.L.P. Chapter 5.

In an article published in *Youth Review* in 1970, Matthew Dieppe,[1] a voluntary worker in a club in the North West describes how the members' committee were encouraged to take an increasing responsibility for all affairs affecting the club. They interviewed applicants for the post of full-time leader as part of a series of interviews by staff, management committee and a consultant group of social workers and had joint consultations with these groups at the time of making a decision and offering the post to one of the applicants. At the time of planning for a new club building this members' committee had a series of meetings with an architect, discussing purpose and function of the club. When they saw the architect's plans drawn *from their brief* they showed disappointment at the unimaginative planning. Now they realized that their ideas were being taken seriously. This increased their confidence. They began to modify their ideas through discussion with other members and visits to other buildings, and the understanding of the architect's role meant that they could present a more demanding but less detailed brief to him, giving him more scope to provide the solutions to their requirements. Finally *their* needs expressed in the brief were realized by the architect's skill in planning and, with only minor modifications, the plans became a reality. Matthew Dieppe says that 'the club has been established after making certain assumptions. . . . The assumption is that the exploration and testing out of situations of authority and control is a fundamental need in adolescence . . .'

The small groups within the total membership have structures and forms of self-government in terms of control, goals and decision-making, and it is in these small groups that opinions about the club as a whole are formed. Decisions made by 'higher' authority affecting the pattern of membership of the club, use of resources, limitations and expectations in relation to the programme, will inevitably be discussed in the small groups and it is here that the real feelings around any decision affecting their membership will be expressed and the group's action or reaction decided. The role of the group worker is seen in his concern with the interplay of members, how infor-

[1] Member Participation in a north-west club: M. Dieppe: *Youth Review*, Spring 1970.

mation is communicated, received and discussed, opinions expressed and formalized into action in accord both with the goals and aspirations of the small group and of the larger group (club). This suggests that the ideal would be an adult worker for each small group and some device whereby all the small groups can feel that their desires and expectations are fully understood and that they are involved in decisions made at a higher level. The objectives can be stated like this:

(*a*) recognizing the strength of relationships in the small group (friendship or activity), encouraging members to express their honest feelings in the atmosphere of security which their group offers:

(*b*) supporting the autonomy of the small groups in the conduct of their affairs:

(*c*) increasing the area of opportunities for members to take part in major decision-making through techniques which bring small groups together in a community of work:

(*d*) enabling minorities, 'low status' and opposition groups to present their case:

(*e*) as members grow in social maturity, affording more opportunities for social responsibility and the establishment of their own authority.

Techniques for Group Decision-making

The two most common forms for group decision-making in organizations is that of a central committee, council or executive made up of representatives of small groups, and the election of a number of members by the total membership. In the former the individuals are elected by the members of *a* group to represent their *sectional interest* and in the latter by a majority of the total membership to represent *all their interests*. The representative-type of decision-making body is a very sophisticated form requiring a great deal of skill on the part of the representatives. A representative of a small group requires a clear brief as to his function in the meeting of the representative body, how far can he express his own feelings or only contribute what he is instructed to say, can he act as he thinks his group would want him to or must he 'refer' back before committing his group. Perhaps the representative elected by the total membership feels it is his right to act as he feels, for how can he act to please all the conflicting sectional interests. As a committee or council is made up of people acting in this way one can only hope that it represents a sample of the desires and expressions of the full membership. 'The creation of effective group government within any representative body will show certain effects of its representative character. This condition will arise because in addition to the usual complexities of interaction between persons, the members are functioning constantly in a kind of three-layer consciousness. They react in terms of their own feelings and opinions, in terms of their constituencies, and in terms of the issues, needs, problems of the representative group itself.'[1] Grace Coyle goes on to add that 'the central body of course develops its own set of personal acceptances and rejections, its own *esprit-de-corps*, and its own programme'. This is to be expected if we accept Homans' hypothesis that[2] 'if the interactions between the members of a group are frequent . . . sentiments of liking will grow up between them, and these sentiments will lead in turn to further interactions . . .' The youth worker needs to recognize what Grace Coyle calls the three layer consciousness which affects the functioning of members of such a representative body and the fact that such a body will acquire certain characteristics of any group where members come together regularly for some common purpose. If he fails to understand this he is likely to see the committee or council as a clique inevitably drawing farther and farther away from the electorate. His function is to help them to see that they will have these problems and to help them identify the difference between their individual and group opinions and those of the rank-and-file and to acquire ways of testing out their proposals inside the total membership before moving to a decision.

There are a number of techniques which can be adopted

[1] *Working with American Youth*: Grace Coyle: (Chapter VIII pp. 156-157).

[2] *The Human Group*: G. C. Homans: Routledge & Kegan Paul 1951.

whereby the full membership is involved in self-government,[1] some of which are in line with the representative-type committee, like the Club Parliament, and others which afford the opportunity to the central committee to test out the feelings and requirements of the full membership, like consensus, referendum opinion polls and forums.

[1] *Self Government in the Youth Group*: J. P. Leighton: N.A.Y.C Pamphlet.

Chapter Seven

Working with Individuals

Discussing the provision of opportunities for 'association' the Albemarle Report saw the coming together of young people with 'understanding and helpful adults' as, amongst other things, an opportunity for counsel and went on to say: 'Only too rarely do young people feel enough confidence in an older and more experienced person to seek advice: parents often prove inadequate or some children are too shy to put to them the difficulties that bear on them most hardly. We believe that the good youth group should try to cater for these needs. . . . There should be nothing in the structure of any organization, however firm in its discipline and its programme, to prevent the officer or leader from being regarded as the natural counsellor to those he leads. . . .'[1] In *Youth and Community Work in the 70's* (para. 242) we read, 'Youth leaders and teachers often help with the "problems" of their charges, although the degree to which they are used and the degree to which advice is taken has always depended on the relationship between the young person and the adult and the regard each has for the other.' Later in the Report (para. 348) we read 'Counselling has always been accepted as part of the work of most youth workers since this is an obvious way of helping young people at this stage of their development.' There is still confusion in the minds of many youth workers about the apparent interchangeability of such terms as helping, counselling, pastoral care, and the claims made that what they refer to is an art, a science, or natural in the very process of living with other people, with the result that a degree of mystique has grown up around the function in the same way that, at an earlier stage, mystique surrounded the term group work.

In the preceding chapter the youth worker was seen as a person who, alone or with other adults, works with small groups within the larger membership which is being helped through

[1] *The Youth Service in England and Wales*: H.M.S.O. 1960. Chapter 5.

group process to achieve certain common goals and a community of work. He is concerned with the autonomous nature of the small groups and a desire for cohesiveness, which may bring conflict and place limitations on the small group, but essential for the continuation of the organization. Through his relationship with the small groups and the skill he brings to them the youth worker helps individuals with their problems experienced in coming to terms with all that goes on in the small group and the organization. These problems are seen by the youth worker as part of his job and he takes them up with the individuals concerned within the normal course of events.[1] However as he continues to work in this way more young people are likely to bring other personal problems to him. The problems which the young person brings to the youth worker may be of a similar nature to those recognized by the worker through his observation and contact with the member as he acts and reacts within the club. However, some of the problems may have no connection with any part of the programme or group experience, and may be to do with his other-group situations such as home, school, work, neighbourhood. They may be to do with his feelings of inadequacies in the various roles he plays or expects to play in the near future, in fact to do with any of the tasks discussed in Chapter Four.

Only recently has the youth worker been induced to examine what this helping really requires of the helper and the person being helped. Previously help, in respect of young people's problems, was almost certainly advice-giving by an adult who through 'experience' had arrived at certain prescriptions which if taken as directed would remedy the problem. This meant that if the person did not accept the advice and follow the instructions he was a fool, stupid, lacking in moral fibre or afraid of the 'medicine'. Naturally if he followed the advice he was a wise, faithful and brave person. There are many professional people who have, or can perform, the helping role as part of their

[1] In *The Youth Worker as a First-Aid Counsellor in Impromptu Situations* (Chester House Publications) George Lovell describes practical ways in which youth workers can help young people to make decisions, choices and satisfactory relationships with other people without providing specific advice and ready-made answers.

profession although it is not their main skill, such as doctors, clergy, solicitors and others who accept that their professional skill is first of all that of helping, such as caseworkers, psychiatrists, group workers, guidance counsellors.

The Helper–Client Relationship

As youth work has developed, agencies have become less involved in meeting the survival or material and physical needs of young people and are more involved in those needs of a secondary nature which arise out of the complexities of an industrial and mass society. Much more now the concern centres around personal relationships and the growing ability to make effective relationships: to help individuals 'achieve a better adjustment between himself and his environment'.[1] The youth worker sees himself working on the creation of relationships through which the individual member can be helped. There are, of course, many forms of relationship having different features and serving different purposes, and we need to look at the features and purposes of the variety of personal relationships any single person engages in, for in this way we differentiate the expectations of those in the relationship and the effectiveness of the relationship. The friendship relationship will be different to the parent–child relationship: to the teacher–child relationship, to the youth worker–member relationship, to the boss–employee relationship, to the wife–husband relationship and so on. The youth worker will not always be seen by members in terms of a counsellor–client role – this 'helping' role he plays at times with some young people – for this grows out of his demonstration of skill in a more generalized role. Usually the member of the organization will have a relationship, of sorts, with the youth worker before he sees him as being useful in a face-to-face counselling role and it is as the members' confidence and trust in the worker grows that he feels able to use the worker in this intimate way. In the club situation the young person may feel that the youth worker sees him first of all as a member, just another member, like the rest in the club and it is only as the worker demonstrates his interest in the member as an individual person and in his total life experiences as well as his club experiences

[1] *The Casework Relationship*: F. P. Biestek: Unwin: Part 1.

that a relationship can begin which affords the opportunity for the member to express his feelings in the knowledge that this person will not judge him, condemn him or be shocked by what is expressed. He will not expect these expressions to alter his 'rights' of membership, as though this function of the worker is outside his function as the club leader. In a sense this is as it should be although the worker may see it as parts of a total function.

There are a number of things which hinder the development of members' confidence and trust in the youth worker as a person concerned with individual persons. The most common being lack of time to devote attention to all the individual needs and problems, but one suspects that this is often an excuse or rationalization. Leaders can create busy-ness, and justify it, in order to avoid personal contact or 'unpleasant' situations. Another is to fail to see and respond to persons as unique individuals needing to be helped to come to terms with a unique set of circumstances (environment). This failure leads to generalizing about behaviour, not attempting to understand behaviour in terms of an individual's social and cultural background and using expressions like 'normal behaviour', 'good' or 'bad' behaviour. If the young person experiences this sort of attitude on the part of the youth worker when he is dealing with the larger group then he is unlikely to see him as an understanding or sympathetic person. The more he sees the youth worker, in his capacity as leader of the club, prescribing 'right' and 'wrong' ways of action for the club as a whole the less he is likely to see him as a person who can help his feelings and his situations. It has been said that young people want a robust relationship with such adults as youth workers and what is meant by this is an honest, frank and challenging relationship. The youth worker who over-identifies with young people will not provide the conditions whereby the individual can be helped to look more realistically at his own situation and become self-determining. Sympathy, which says, 'I feel so sorry for you in this condition that I weep with you', offers nothing in helping the individual to do something positive about his condition. Empathy is much more positive because it expresses compassion, is more realistic and less emotionally charged. Naturally the youth worker feels emotionally for the young people with whom he associates regularly, this feeling is part of the relationship, but it needs to be controlled. There was a time when it was thought that a case-worker or social worker should not be emotionally involved in the client's problem and this led to the accusation that such workers were too clinical and cold. There is an emotional aspect in all relationships, some of those mentioned earlier will have a greater emotional basis than others, some are based on emotion and often individuals have to seek help from others not so emotionally involved as their partner. The youth worker knows that many of the growing-up and searching for independence problems of the adolescent are brought to him because the young person feels he cannot discuss these with his parents, often because of the strong emotional content in the parent–child relationship. Here, then, he is looking for someone who is empathetic but not so emotionally involved that he is unable to help. But there will still be an emotional warmth in the worker–member relationship.

What it Means to Ask for Help

The person who is in a position to play a helping role needs to understand what it means to seek help from another person, help, that is, to do with change rather than help which is the seeking of information or receiving material benefit. Almost everyone who has played the helping role will agree that early in the consultation the person presenting the problem will give the impression that the need is for others to adjust to the situation rather than the client, or that there would be no problem if the conditions of the situation were different, or he seeks approval of his feelings. Much of this suggests that, intolerable though the present situation is, it is to be favoured above any new situation which might arise from any action taken by the client. Most of us fear change and the more unknown the realms we may have to experience if we decide to 'change our ways' the more likely we are to find reasons not to take action and remain in the known, albeit unsatisfactory, situation which has prompted the call for help. The elements in the process may be likened to those which the Church labels repentance, confession, submission and Faith.[1] Alan Keith-Lucas says what it really takes

[1] *The Art and Science of Helping*: Alan Keith-Lucas in Case Conference Vol 13. No. 5. 1966.

to ask for help is:

1. 'A recognition that there is something wrong, and that one cannot do anything about it oneself, without taking help, that is.

2. 'A willingness to confess this weakness to another, to let him know what one really is.

3. 'A willingness to let him advise one, to have some power over one's life.

4. 'Finally, a willingness to risk the unknown – to give up one's present situation, however intolerable this may be, for some unknown that may look better but may actually turn out worse.'

This is difficult for all men but in one respect the adolescent may be less fearful of the consequences of change than the adult, for all about him is change. As we have said earlier the adolescent is going through a total process of change from dependence to independence, establishing a self, testing out beliefs, in fact he is seldom satisfied with his present position and retaining what is and more likely trying to reach deeper meaning to his life. Youth workers talk about young people 'testing-out' relationships, 'seeing how far they can go' with the worker and the organization and it is around these situations that the youth worker can *offer* help, not expecting the young person to gain great insights but offering something which may not be available elsewhere, the opportunities for testing-out thoughts and feelings and being helped to look at these within a trusting, loving and on-going relationship – on-going for as long as the young person wants it to be so.

What it Means to Offer Help

More often than not when help is required we think in terms of giving rather than offering. It is not just a semantic argument when we discuss the differences between giving and offering. Giving tends to presuppose a relation of superior–inferior or authority–subservience. James Baldwin discussing the American Negro 'problem', comments on the attitudes underlying the expressions of some 'white' Americans who desire to give the 'black' American equality and freedom. By what divine right is it theirs to give, he asks, and suggests that all they can really do is 'set us free'.[1] Giving suggests that for some reasons the giver is better able, in a more favoured position, to understand and solve someone else's problem. It suggests a one-solution-type response rather than opening-up dialogue around a number of possible solutions and there is always a tendency for the solution to be as the adviser sees the problem rather than as the client sees and feels it. Of course the client can accept or reject what is being given, but what happens to the relationship if it is rejected and what value is it to the client if accepted? Offering carries the same process of acceptance or rejection but the person helping builds the relationship starting from the premise that it is a fundamental right of the person seeking help to be free to choose the action he will take. In fact the helper can only maintain a relationship through which further help is possible if he accepts this, for this sort of help is to do with the client's choices and continuing discussion of the consequences of those choices. *The help we are talking about here is in the manner it is offered rather than what is offered.* Choices cannot be presented in such a manner that the client has no alternative, it cannot be forced on a person through exhortation or techniques of persuasion. The answer to the client's question 'what shall I do?' may be met by the helper but how he responds to this must be free of compulsion. Christ's answer to the wealthy young ruler's question 'How shall I inherit the Kingdom of God?' was, give up what you have and follow me, change your present situation and have faith in what follows. And he went away feeling the price was too high. He was not 'powered' into making the 'right' choice.

The person offering help must be aware of his own responses to human situations and how he is seen by other people. This is not an easy task, for how can we be really certain that we know how others see us? But he can recognize his feelings about a number of human conditions, such as his feeling of impatience or sympathy with the weak, toleration of uncertainty, disgust with inefficiency and become aware of his biases and prejudices.

[1] *The Fire Next Time*: and: *Notes to a Native Son*: J. Baldwin: M. Joseph (1964).

He needs to convey his desire to treat this person and his problem as unique and not as a case no matter how similar the conditions may be to others. The atmosphere of whatever form the helping sessions take must be one of ease, aiming at a reduction of the tension and anxiety which prevents the client expressing his feelings, both positive and negative. Keith Lucas says, 'it is usually true that *people need a great deal more help with their negative feelings than with their positive . . .' and goes on to say, 'the helping relationship must be one in which negative feelings can be expressed without fear of blame, anger, sorrow or loss of face*'[1] (his italics). Although this person has sought help he should not be seen by the person offering the help as dependent or 'helpless' or even as a weak person. The helping person supports the need of the one helped to be accepted as *a* person with weaknesses, but also with some strengths, may be displaying more dependence than independence at the moment. In this he upholds or helps restore the dignity and feeling of worth of this person. The helper must respect the confidential nature of what transpires when he is playing this role and not use information for other purposes, as Father Biestek says 'He (the client) does not want to exchange his reputation for the help he will receive. . . .'[2] The youth leader who plays this role needs to be careful that he does not break this confidence when, in other club situations, he is playing a similar but slightly different role with the groups where the client is also a member. He must be aware of his own limitations within the helping process. What he is not, is as important as what he is. He may not have the training or the professional standing to deal totally with certain problems. Knowing when the situation calls for other forms of help which can be offered by other people and how to help the client see this, is part of his skill. The more the helper can demonstrate his caring for the client as a person the more the client will recognize the need for help from other sources.

The Christian youth worker may feel that his beliefs cannot be divorced from the helping role. He may feel that the sole purpose of his counselling or helping is to bring young people to a commitment to Christ. In a sense there is an unavoidable

[1] *The Art and Science of Helping*: A. Keith-Lucas: Case Conference Vol. 13. No. 5. 1966.

[2] *The Casework Relationship*: F. P. Biestek: Unwin: Part 1.

directiveness about any form of helping if only because the helper cannot be passive or neutral, certainly he is likely to 'pass on' to the client his notion that caring for others is worthwhile, a healthier state than not caring, and this is a moral issue. The very fact that he upholds the uniqueness of man and his rights to self-determination, and his demonstration of acceptance of all conditions of men must be suggesting some direction, taking some moral stand. However, the Christian youth worker has to be clear about his total role and his agency's expectations and the ways in which the members will view him in his several functions. Naturally it may be made known to the members that one of the objects, or the ultimate goal, of the organization is to bring young people to a commitment to Christ. This may condition who will, or can, seek membership and such young people may expect the youth worker to play a pastoral-counselling role. On the other hand the agency may not be so explicit about its objectives or see its task as helping young people to such a specific commitment, in which case the young people who accept membership will not expect, necessarily, the youth worker to play the role of pastoral-counsellor although they may well want him to function as a counsellor![1]

Halmos says: 'All human relationships cause those, who take part in them, to assume the characteristics of each other, and the counselling relationship has this nature too, which is enhanced by the therapeutic intentions of the counsellor.' It cannot be over-stressed that, in the main, the club leader is seen by the members as a person of authority necessary for the total function of 'club-leading'. The leader may have much skill to offer in helping individuals with their individual problems but this is something the young people discover through association and the forming of a relationship through the general function of the leader. Seldom does the member 'join' the club because he sees the need for a counsellor–client relationship around a particular problem. Before the individual member seeks out the club-leader, or other club worker, to play the role of helping in the intimate sense of counselling, he will have made some judgements about this person. He will have ideas about the youth worker's 'line', his ability to be objective, to listen and be

[1] *The Faith of the Counsellors*: Paul Halmos: Constable: Chapter 5.

understanding, not condemning the person because of his state at the moment, in fact, about his helpfulness. Some of the things the youth worker stands for and believes are good for all men, will have been demonstrated in the general work of the club. It may be these demonstrations which attract the individual to seeing the youth worker as a person who will offer help with his individual problems. The opposite may also be felt by the member. He may feel that the youth worker's own personal convictions would be far too directive, that all he could offer was *a* final solution. The Christian youth worker may be in the same dilemma as the clergyman in this respect, as Kathlene Heasman says: 'In his own pastoral work a clergyman is operating on a common ground of belief and commitment and is the leader and guide to those to whom he ministers. As a counsellor, however, he is in a different role, and this may present some difficulty. In his counselling capacity he has to help, support and comfort the person within the orbit of the person's own thoughts, feelings and beliefs which may not necessarily coincide with his own as a clergyman. As a counsellor his own religious convictions should not intrude upon the counselling interviews any more than his political beliefs. Yet he may feel that he is failing in his duties as a priest if he does not introduce what he believes is essential. The only answer one can give to this is that if the clergyman or minister intends to put over his own religious convictions, this should be made quite clear to the person from the outset, and should this not be acceptable then the person should be referred to someone else.'

However, if the young person uses that part of the youth worker's skill we are discussing here, it is more than likely that he has taken into consideration the convictions of the youth worker and made some assessment as to how these will intervene in the helping process. A bigger problem is that of knowing, or not knowing, how many young people feel unable to use this part of the worker's skill because of his convictions. At all times the person playing the helping role will have before him the idea of non-directiveness as a guide and this alone will help him to keep his intervention within bounds, but his very approach through caring and loving, his concern for this person, his dedication to the problem, his support of self-determination spring from some inner, moral or spiritual conviction and this will condition his responses. Some of this will be 'rubbed-off' by the person being helped in the process.

Problems of the Individual Member

The sort of problems which are presented to people who play the helping role are often peculiar to an age group or stage of development. Most of the problems of the adolescent centre around the growth tasks outlined in Chapter Three. No matter how common, they will be seen as peculiar to the individual. Perhaps the most usual one is expressed by the young person as 'they do not understand'. He sees himself as misunderstood by his parents, teachers, adults at work, in fact by adults in general. Often this is a confession of not being able to understand himself. He does not always seek out the youth worker to make this statement in confidence, more likely it is expressed within the safety and approval of his group. The youth worker may employ skill at such times with the group, helping them to express their feelings and produce examples or evidence of this lack of understanding on the part of adults. At some stage in such discussions – usually one-sided – some young people will comment on the inability to discuss the subject with the adults involved because 'they don't listen', 'they don't give us the chance to explain', 'they say we are ungrateful' and other generally accepted comments. But within this the youth worker can discern differences and other problems within the generalized one as demonstrated by the expressions of some individuals about their parents, teachers, bosses rather than the less specific 'they'. Some of these will form the starting point of a continuing dialogue with individual members about their conflict with parents over discipline, authority, leisure-time pursuits, associations, appearance, work, what they see as important in life, or not merely the opposite of this, but lack of any show of caring what the young person does with his life, or inconsistency and ambivalence. It is from the same sanctuary of 'his' group that the young person shows his anxiety about a whole range of concerns common to adolescents. Such as sexual relationships, authority in general and of the agents of the law in particular, moral values, standards and double-standards, adequacy or inadequacy, frustrations – certainly to do with delaying immediate gratification for the promise of something finer later on.

When the individual approaches the youth worker after the group discussion to follow-up points which affect him personally he expects the youth worker to play a different role to the one he played in the group setting.

From time to time the youth worker is requested to help with a problem of deeper concern because the member is in trouble with the law, has been turned out of home, wishes to break-off an undesirable relationship, is having 'serious sex-problems'. The problem has to be heard and follow-up will depend on the nature of the problem, but the helper will need to decide whether he can deal with the condition adequately. If not, he has to help the young person to see that other professional help is needed, and in some cases essential. This latter is not just a bald statement as though washing one's hands of the whole affair, it is done retaining the relationship which may still be used by the young person.

There is also the helping role which is more like advice-giving. Young people approach youth workers on a number of matters affecting their progress at school, work, the pursuit of skills, further education, some of which lead to discussion of personal relationships and problems of 'loyalties', choice and their consequences, and some concerned with seeking information or using the adult as a sounding board. Advice-giving has to be approached with care. Obviously there are occasions when the advice is factual and could be given by anyone who knows. There is also advice-giving which is centred on a problem, the 'what would you do if you were me in this situation' type of request for guidance. The person being asked for help comes up with a solution, or perhaps alternatives. The disadvantages here are that the person seeking guidance is not helped to identify desirable goals for himself and relies on the helper to do this; an assumption that the helper knows all there is to know about the person being helped, including how he will re-act or adjust to the new situation assuming he takes the advice; emphasis is put on making a particular choice by the person helping and this may lead to further anxiety states if the person being helped does not have satisfying experiences when following-up the choice. This kind of helping is fairly common and very much so in advice-giving to the young, whether asked for or not. It is the sort of advice which is prefixed by 'well, if

I were you . . .', and we are back to those things mentioned earlier in this chapter, of one person in a superior position giving something to someone in an inferior position. It relies heavily on the experience, status and supposed wisdom of the adult, simply because he is an adult. How far the advice offered (information giving is different) is really helpful is questionable. But some young people, because of their inability to express themselves or fear of self-examination and lack of faith in themselves, may rely on this advice-giving type of helping, are happier when someone else is making decisions and routeing their life for them. It may be necessary for the helper to carry this responsibility for some young people as a temporary measure. Survival needs are not only to do with the material things of life, there are psychological and social survival needs, and the youth worker may need to give a great deal of support to some young people, which may mean directing certain decision-making. But he must always have the other ideal of self-determination in mind and through his contact with the individual he must be helping him to accept more responsibility for decision-making, for running his own life in the belief that 'he is endowed by the Creator with a fundamental, inalienable right to choose and decide the appropriate means for the attaining of his own personal destiny'[1] and the appropriate means are those of the person being helped not of the helper. It can be painful to the helper when he sees the appropriate means are self-destructive and he may have to take some responsibility for decision-making because he believes that the person being helped does not have the capacity to act for himself, at the moment. There is a need to distinguish between those single acts following decisions made by the client which the helper thinks are unwise but are not beyond retrieving and those which are moving into the realms of 'illness' where the helping person feels that the client needs protection from his confusion and incapacity to deal with his emotional, mental or physical state. This will require skill in sustaining the relationship between the helper and the helped; in knowing the sources of help available through other agencies, and in helping the client to see the need for other sources of help and assisting him to make the contact.

[1] *The Casework Relationship*: F. P. Biestek: Chapter 6.

This chapter may have done nothing to clarify the confusion mentioned at the beginning, it may have added to it, for it may be that we are, as yet unable to define the words counselling and helping with any clarity in terms of a discipline. Words have to be borrowed from those professions which are concerned with helping people, from case-work, group work, the Church, medicine, welfare work, but helping is much wider than any of these professions and is being 'taken-up' by all sorts of people who have to deal with people no matter what the end-product or primary task of the organization happens to be. It is almost inevitable that there will be, for a time at least, an interchangeability of terms when people are talking about the process of one person helping another. What is important is that the terms be understood in the context in which they are being used and an attempt made to understand what precisely helping counselling, pastoral counselling, involve in practice. Youth workers are being helped to recognize a number of skills within their total function, namely social group work skill, counselling skill, community work skills and, common to all these, management or administrative skill. A worker's strength, skill-wise, may be in any one or more of these skills and he may have pursued some training either full-time, part-time or in-service in any one or more of these skills. As far as case-work counselling or individual helping is concerned he may have had training as a Counsellor; been introduced to some of the principles and methods of counselling within a generic youth course; or more often, discussed his handling of 'individual' problems with some adults in his agency, local Youth Officer or other club leaders. Many club leaders will recognize that they have been used as the helping person and, as said earlier, will have assumed that this is inherent in the role of club leader or youth worker. Like much of his work he has acted from his own convictions and feelings, somewhat intuitively, without the opportunity of testing out his work with a body of knowledge represented by a training agency or through regular supervision. The attempt in this chapter has been to give some meat to the bare bones of being helpful, to identify both the art and science involved, and whilst using references to works on Counselling there is no claim that this chapter should be seen as a chapter on counselling. There will be those youth workers and leaders who wish to go deeper into the subject of counselling as they may wish to do with social group work and community work. Some understanding of all these skills is generic to the overall function of the youth worker of today. In some situations one or more adults with a special skill may be employed to meet the special needs of a number of young people. More and more organizations are seeing the need to employ a counsellor whose function is counselling and where it is known that this service is available not only for those in regular membership but for any young person who feels more comfortable in taking his problems to this organization because he thinks his problem is not severe enough to take to other agencies or he cannot identify an agency which will deal with his problem. Increasingly, but slowly, a number of agencies are being established exclusively as counselling centres for the young.

The majority of club leaders, however, will be called upon to help individual club members with a whole range of adolescent problems. In using the term helping-role in respect of this part of his function there is no desire to belittle its importance in comparison to the different or deeper skill of the Counsellor.

Chapter Eight

PROGRAMME PLANNING

We come, now, to the question of what constitutes programme, what is it that is offered for the members' satisfaction or gratification and how is programme or activity measured and evaluated in terms of the groups and the individuals needs, the purpose of youth work and the particular agency's ethos and method. A number of statements made or implied in earlier chapters need to be re-stated and examined.

1. Generally the purpose of youth work is seen as aiding the development of young people. Adults responsible for agency policy will state aims idealistically, that is, that through some form of association and guidance by an adult or team of adults young people will benefit physically, mentally and particularly socially and move towards an 'acceptable' maturity.

2. Young people are more generally concerned with immediate gratification in their association with others and through activity and are unable, or do not desire, to see their activities as means to ends expressed in idealistic terms.

3. There is likely to be simply expressed (avowed) reasons for joining a group or club but the unavowed, non-expressed needs of the individual will become apparent to the youth worker through group inter-action and the member's feelingof gratification will increase if both are being met. We can think of needs in terms of satisfactions and each member has a number of satisfactions to be met through his membership of the particular organization he chooses to join. If we see the organization as having something to offer to those who use it, those adults who 'purvey' the something have to develop ways or techniques of knowing what the needs of the customers or clients are; how these are met or unmet by the environment or the other group experiences: the process pursued by the client before he chooses to use the services of the organization: how he then uses those services and for what satisfactions; the experiences he has whilst using the services including the influences of his peers in the way

they perceive the organization and its services. So programme planning begins with some analysis like this!

1. Identify needs:
   (*a*) of the adolescent in general terms of developmental tasks,
   (*b*) of the particular young people in terms of individual needs.

2. Recognize that these needs can be satisfied in a variety of ways:
   (*a*) through other groups' affiliations and agencies,
   (*b*) through a variety of means (activity in its broadest sense) within a single organization or agency,
   (*c*) that satisfaction gained in one organization or agency does not exclude similar satisfactions being achieved in a different setting or organization.

3. Realize the limitations of the organization:
   (*a*) all of a person's satisfactions cannot be met by one organization or agency,
   (*b*) concentrate on those satisfactions it can provide,
   (*c*) use scarce resources in manpower, time, material and finance to the best advantage.

Continually the youth worker must ask himself 'what sort of business am I in' or 'what is it I am offering these particular young people'. If it is true, and if we believe it desirable, that youth work is client-centred and concerned with trying to meet young people's needs then we are concerned with client-satisfaction. Young people may well be less concerned with the intrinsic value of certain forms of activity than with what it can do for them in terms of satisfactions, such as, being needed, belonging, gaining status and regard. The worker needs to be aware of changes in the environment if he is to approach programme planning realistically. By this, I mean, an awareness of how young people perceive the programme, the values they put on various kinds of activity, many of which they can pursue or see pursued at a higher level or in more sophisticated settings than attempted in the youth club. Youth workers react strongly when one suggests that they are in a competitive market and that their 'selling' approaches have to be carefully studied and the techniques of 'selling' what they have to offer improved. Yet youth work is in competition with many other agencies, undertakings, attractions and ideologies. It may well believe that it has something particular to offer to young people, something which may not be available to some young people in any one other institution or sphere of social living, and if this is so, bewailing the fact that only a minority of those who may benefit from the service do so, does not produce solutions.

It may well be that what the Youth Service has to offer in terms of end-product or ultimate goal in social education is badly 'packaged' so that the means through which the goal may be achieved are no longer appropriate to many young people. Alternatively, there may be only one type of 'package' which appeals to certain 'buyers', and we may need to produce a number of different 'packages' for buyers with different needs, with different sorts of satisfactions. Using the notion of having a commodity to sell, maybe we are trying to sell an out-dated product, one which does not now provide satisfactions. This can apply equally to parts of the programme. Some activity attracts a number of members – it may happen by design or fortuitously – and in pursuing it they gain certain satisfactions, it may reach saturation point in gratification, but then members may find other means of gaining the same satisfactions or feel that there is little need to go on having satisfactions met. At this stage their participation in the activity begins to wane and the adults concerned with programme planning are tempted to find ways of 'propping-up' the activity, to keep it in existence because it was once successful. Appeals are made to the members loyalty or there is recourse to other coercive methods to keep the activity alive. Naturally there is concern because money has been expended on equipment, plans made covering a long period to accommodate the activity, possibly outside expertise has been engaged. Perhaps the youth worker should give more thought to the satisfactions sought by young people than to the maintenance of the vehicles through which they gain their satisfactions. The vehicles are means and not ends and from time to time they have to be abandoned in preference to new vehicles which attract and hold people's interests as long as they meet the need, but in turn may have to be abandoned.

Before any young person joins a youth group or any activity which is part of the total programme he will have pursued a number of processes. Accepting that he has needs which he seeks to satisfy he is open to influence through a number of techniques which seek to attract him with offers of need satisfaction. The youth service tends to have a poor 'selling' image, in fact its ways of communicating what it has to offer are extremely poor. Perhaps the most successful method of recruiting people to a service or to the purchase of goods, is through recommendation by satisfied clients, but unsatisfied clients will influence prospective clients adversely. The adolescent peer group and other reference groups, such as family, school, play an important part in this pre-decision period. Both the generalized adolescent peer groups and the localized peer groups attitudes are important. The former may have an influence militating against the individual's possible choice to associate with the youth service or any particular organization, in a very general sense, whilst the latter will depend on experiences of local units some of which will support the former, some going contrary to this because their particular satisfactions are being or have been, met by the organization. The prospective client will have gone through a process of comparing what the various agencies have to offer him and not only youth service agencies. but other commercial and non-commercial leisure-time agencies. A similar process occurs in respect of choice within the total programme of the club. What the individual chooses to do depends on the range of choices available to him, his particular needs and how he sees these being satisfied by the different activities available; the influence of his immediate group of friends and other reference groups and his experiences of similar activities.

Having made his choice and gained membership does not end the process. He will be concerned, now, about his choice, was it the right one, how far has he committed himself, what are the consequences of such commitment and some of these anxieties will be added to by the experiences and expressions of others both within the organization and those outside it. And again this applies to the thing as a whole and to his choices of commitment to activities within the programme. A good example of this is the member who chooses to 'run' for a place on the committee.

He can be put under pressure by his friendship group who see him moving away from them and identifying with the power-structure, yet others, not of his friendship group, may resist his attempts to join the 'elite' for a number of reasons. On joining the organization the young person may have immediate feelings of gratification through the process of initiation, that is, where the organization is geared to receive newcomers with enthusiasm and care and so the newcomer has 'good' feelings or dispositions towards the organization and the significant persons in it. But this caring for newcomers tends to fall away rather quickly and people go back to their groupings, associations and functions which occupied them before the newcomer arrived. In some cases the newcomer is previously associated with members or can quickly identify with a group, but there are others who may not be in this fortunate or sophisticated situation and maybe the inability to socialize easily and comfortably with their peers is the unavowed reason for seeking membership. If this is not understood then their post-joining feelings are not being met, anxieties added to and deepened and their departure is not one of positive healthy choice but negative and possibly damaging. This can be true, also in respect of the smaller groups of more intimate activity within the organization as a whole.

To Whom is the Agency's Operation Aimed?

As stated at the beginning of this chapter the needs of the adolescent cannot be wholly met by one means. The youth service, or the Youth and Community Service, has its main operation directed at young people although it now realizes the problems inherent in thinking of young people's needs being met through an overall programme which separates them from other age groups. Nevertheless, under this ever broadening canopy, agencies choose to focus their work on specific needs or groups of young people. One of the criticisms we have made of the club in this country is its tendency to be too general in approach as though it is all things to all young people in leisure-time. It is fairly clearly observable that some agencies' methods or organization indicate their specific goals and to a large degree determine the programme content, such as the uniformed organizations, Young Farmers' Clubs, Guilds, and the more recent service to the community organizations. Sponsoring agencies inevitably determine, if only partially, methods of work and therefore programme content. For some young people there is a need to add to their immediate gratification of belonging to the local, small unit or group, the feeling of belonging and identification with a movement which is national or even world-wide, albeit in rather abstract and ideological terms. Such organizations incorporate a system of awards marking progress in activities which are common to all units in the organization. Another method of reinforcing goals employed by organizations with affiliated groups is the district, regional and national programme of events, conferences, courses to which local units send their representatives, in many cases as a reward for service or progress within the local unit or group. How such programmes are used will determine whether they are 'good', that is, in line with the aim of helping young people to be self-directing towards social action for change within their own organization and society in general, or 'bad' in that young people become 'fodder' for the inculcation of ideologies which are not aimed at desirable social goals but at retaining the *status quo* or the destruction of society.

The sponsors of the local youth group which may have a strong affiliation with a national agency have to ask more often than those sponsors of the local unit of a national organization, 'to whom are operations aimed'? This must be measured against the resources and the limitations available or possible. A number of fundamental questions have to be discussed:

1. What are the needs we have to meet? How have these been expressed and by whom? The Church may feel a need to offer something to young people, or some young people, for a number of reasons. It may feel it has a duty to offer a service although similar services, clubs and youth organizations, are available in the community, because it believes that young people should have an opportunity to accept or reject the challenge of the Church; it may recognize a gap in the services to young people in the neighbourhood and want to provide some means of filling that gap: it may be responding to the wishes of young people or the church members.
2. What have we got to offer? Is it something specific or can young people obtain it elsewhere? What would be different

about content and method in what we have to offer? What is our goal, what are our motives for wanting to sponsor such a a service?

3. To whom would we be offering this service? Should we aim at a particular clientele? Are we going to concentrate on a particular group or social group? What other services are in the 'market'? Shall we be duplicating what exists? Are there groups within the neighbourhood whose needs are not being met by existing agencies? These questions lead to some decision about who needs a service.
4. How would we offer the service? This follows from the previous questions as to who is in need. At this stage the sponsors are shaping, in theory, a particular service and it may be that what is now seen as necessary is a counselling, non-membership type of service, or a social club, or a special interest club or groups – one or the other or perhaps all of them.
5. Which do we choose and how do we establish it? By now in the thinking-through process there are limited objectives which should allow the sponsors to go for particular needs, perhaps of particular young people, in a purposive and concentrated way.

The type of club or service perceived through an approach like this should have fairly clear goals which will give direction to the youth workers who will be engaged to carry out the functions of the sponsoring agency. It will also give some direction to the type of programme of the unit, club or service.

Whether the agency goals and the age group or needs suggest the establishment of an organization which follows, adopts or adapts a nationally formulated programme in the widest possible terms, or is much more localized and *ad hoc*, the youth worker will expect to be able to encourage the young people who choose to use the agency's service to be critical of the stated goals and to shape the internal programme content within the external system. He will see the goals of the agency being achieved by young people who use the activity content in an exploratory and dynamic way. It would be contrary to his skill and understanding if the young people were expected to follow uncritically, without question some prescribed routine of activities laid down by his agency. The stimuli in programme content comes from many sources, including the agency and the worker, but these are presented as opportunities around which the young people exercise choice. The objective of the worker is to widen the range of choices both in activity and the way they are conducted, but in all this he is concerned with the group's move to self-direction and self-government in the belief that people are capable of choosing what is ethically good for themselves and others, that where they are involved in decision-making they will choose to do what is in the best interests of the community or group and where people gain satisfaction from achieving small tasks they are encouraged to take on bigger ones. Incentives are a proper concern of the youth worker, and whilst adults may debate the worth of competition, awards, and all the status-giving symbols as being desirable or undesirable, his concern is seeing 'below the symptomatic behaviour to the underlying emotional results. Not the winning of a badge as such nor the acquiring of a skill, but the place of this experience in the life situation of the member . . .'[1] This points to the danger of generalizing about competition and gaining awards as being something that young people enjoy or do not enjoy. For some, having feelings of failure in other spheres of their life, competition may be absolute anathema or an opportunity to feel success, for others it may be the only way they can feel accepted, ways of satisfying their power-want, a 'cover-up' for other feelings of inadequacy. Yet others may have no great need to attach significance to winning and receiving acclaim. The worker will consider effects on the individuals before he introduces or encourages this sort of element to activity. Often it may be beyond his control, particularly where he does not wish to veto the beginning of self-programming, but he must always be ready to discuss possible consequences with the group and may have to act independently to protect or support an individual who may be affected adversely by such an element in activity. Competition and rewards do not only come through the more usual games or badge schemes. There will be competition of a different nature in many youth groups where the rewards are less materialistic or obvious. For instance there may well be competition for positions in the hierarchial structure of

[1] *Group Work with American Youth* – Grace Coyle – Harper & Row, 1948.

the group which brings privilege, such as, being a committee member, a leader of a group, those positions which are seen as 'positive' by adults and most members, and, perhaps equally, those positions seen as 'negative' which demand time and attention by the youth worker and his staff. If we construct a graph of members showing their degree of conformity alongside staff-member-contact time we note a disproportionate time spent with those at the top and bottom of the graph, a small percentage of the total membership. The question arises how do those in the middle react to this and how do they compete for staff-member-contact time? Those members at the top of the scale will be afforded opportunities as representatives of the club at area and regional meetings, conferences and courses to further or reinforce their experiences of worth. Sometimes this is motivated by the youth worker in the best interests of the member, sometimes selection of who should attend such functions is based on a different set of criteria, such as other people's impressions of the club or the youth worker as seen through the behaviour and attitudes of the member-representative, and in this case it is doubtful whether the needs of the young person are considered or met. In either case how do those young people who have not and may not reach the pinnacle of approval as represented by being a member of the 'top ten', gain these sorts of experiences? If they are desirable experiences for young people the worker needs to have some procedures within the overall programme that allows for the majority (if not all) to have the opportunities of representation.

Programme Evaluation – by Members

Girls may regard a club differently to boys but it is a mistake to think that their satisfactions can only be gained through some particular girls' programme. Anyone who has spent time in club work will have heard or asked the question 'what do you do with the girls?' There are a number of fairly common statements which denigrate girls and by implication, suggest there are no problems with boys in respect of participation or meeting their needs through club life. Even the belief that girls are more interested in people and boys in things tend to separate them in terms of how they will function within the club. Certainly it is easier to occupy young male adolescents in sporting activities and manual hobbies, but this tends to presuppose that girls are not interested in sports or hobbies. Worse than this it seems to suggest the only solution is to occupy the girl in those activities which she is supposed to be good at, such as, serving in the coffee bar and similar domestic chores. Apart from this they are dismissed as being 'interested only in dancing and boys'. In a study entitled 'Girls at Leisure' Jalna Hanmer says 'Girls seem to regard a club as a place where they can meet their friends, make new friends and engage in activities that both further this purpose and offer new experiences. To the girls, social programme seems to offer the most scope for meeting and making friends . . .' and in answering the charge that 'when boys and girls are together the programme is ruined' she says 'girls do not share this view and seem to think that the programme begins with association. This conflict becomes acute with the older girls, who particularly resent efforts to curtail "meeting and mixing with boys", either directly or by emphasis on a type of programme which does not facilitate this. While relationships are important to girls, this may be in part because they have difficulties with them. They do not seem to be as highly regarded as boys in clubs, and if their wish to associate is undervalued and even, at times, actively opposed, they do have a problem with relationships.' The girls interviewed in this study put outings, dancing, music at the top of their list of things they like to do. Outings are a way of giving satisfaction in the area of meeting new people and offering new experiences but the girls interviewed thought that insufficient outings were arranged for them. Obviously dancing and music is an outlet for their emotions and satisfies the feelings of freedom and well-being. Another important factor in the study was the girls' expression of interest in a wide range of activities many of them not thought of as 'girls activities' but interests they shared with boys, such as football, motor bikes, billiards, snooker. What this study indicates is the importance of opportunities for association as a basis for further experiences. The Albemarle Report, proposing a tripartite objective of association, challenge and training, suggested that association in itself might be meaningless and young people seem to indicate that they desire an extension of this into something they perceive purposive, giving satisfactions and opening up new ways of meeting those satisfactions. Bernard

Davies in an article published in *Youth Review* (Spring 1969) entitled 'Activity in Youth Work: analysing its use and impact' says 'Starting with young people's interests and friendships might be an essential educational principle: but being too satisfied with those interests and friendships, hesitating to offer openings for new experiences and relationships is tantamount to abdicating all responsibility'. The function of the youth worker in relation to the use of whatever is 'programme' is neither one of direction, that is, selecting what is believed to be good experiences for young people for this presupposes some particular responses, or one of absolute permissiveness which is really to abrogate his responsibility. As we see in the example of the football group in Chapter Seven the youth worker is using programme, in this case the activity is football, to help the participants to get greater joy and satisfaction from the game, but also he has another task, concerned with the relationships within the group, attitudes towards authority, individual differences in need of fulfilment and anything that may arise through the interactions within the group and between the particular group (activity) and other groups within the larger club. The particular worker in this situation would have found it difficult not to operate at these two levels because his training helped him to see that in such situations, individuals have 'bundles of satisfactions' not single ones and that one can seldom satisfy the one – the improvement of football skill, for instance – if the other feelings of worth, status, acceptance, dignity, etc. – are not being satisfactorily met. It is interesting to note that the girls mentioned in the Jalna Hanmer study were 'keen on outings' whether they took part in them or not. What appears to give them satisfaction is (*a*) to know that something is happening (*b*) to be involved no matter how remotely or superficially in the planning and preparation (*c*) the knowledge that some of their friends are benefiting from the experience and (*d*) that such experiences become talking points later, so that, even if they have not been on the outing, they get a kind of reflected pleasure from their contemporaries' experiences. Boredom is the thing young people fear most in club programmes and it may be that what brings about the boredom is not seeing the purpose of the activities or of the parts of the whole, in any progression or direction. 'It's the same old routine every night', 'we never do anything exciting', 'you get browned off seeing the same faces night after night', 'there are too many restrictions' are some of the remarks of club members answering the question 'what do you dislike most about your club?' From these and similar remarks made by young people we can deduce a number of factors about programme content as perceived by them rather than how adults would like it to be perceived. Many of the stock activities in clubs are in fact very restrictive. Equipment purchased for specific purposes or space marked and allocated for certain activities are seldom seen as resources which, with a little imagination can be used in a variety of different ways. Excitement can be created by adaptation and innovation and different grouping of people can be influenced to use such equipment and space for pleasure. It is around some of these stock-in-trade activities that one finds restrictions brought about by rules of the game, how the activity should be carried out in a formalized way, through the control exercised by a group who build-up a prior claim because they wish to pursue the activity for which the equipment was purchased or space originally marked. For instance, the table tennis equipment becomes sacrosanct and is used only for the formalized game as we know it and often only by those who already have skill and form some sort of 'inner-club' controlling its use. Seldom is it used for the enjoyment of others who may not wish to be part of the table tennis activity group and yet there are a number of games that can be played around and across the table where more people are engaged and which provide a great deal of fun and satisfaction if only for a few minutes. 'All-in' table tennis, where as many as can get round the table join in, picking up a bat, hitting the ball across the net and then moving on to join the queue at the other end of the table, can be hilarious fun. Another example can be taken from the formalized approach to art. The less formality, or adherence to rules of perspective or copying a model and the more freedom in expression and method the more exciting it will be for many, in fact the wider range of materials used and the ways in which they can be used the more are likely to be attracted and the more experimentation is possible. To see a group of older club members whose previous experiences of art were highly formalized and restricted at school enjoying the sensations of feeling paint as they mixed colours and applied it with fingers, hands and feet to a large 'canvas' of thick brown paper is to realize that this is exciting, a new experience and that they are discovering form where none existed before. Their subsequent art exhibition would have attracted little positive response from many adults but it had done a great deal for the participants. What the experience had done for them is more important than what the activity is. Other examples of the different purposes or satisfactions gained in activity come readily to mind. Drama may be highly formalized and controlled when used for play production but 'informal' and less controlled when used for free expression, for the purpose of the experiences and satisfactions gained in improvisation, with no end-product in the sense of preparing a finished production for public display. Dancing, likewise, can be both formal and controlled where the participants are keen to make progress in performance, learning more dances, preparing for medal tests, and social where it is used for different purposes, providing opportunities for free expression, for the release of emotions, gaining confidence or an attribute which 'opens doors' to other social-function situations. Joy can be experienced by the participants whatever approach is used or for whatever purpose the individuals are using the formalized or less formalized situation. It is not an either-or approach to activity, it is both according to need satisfaction. Young people will expect the formal and controlled activity in order to gain skill in a particular activity whilst desiring the less formal and controlled approach in other activities. Rewards, then, are seen as being different kinds and very much in line with the notion of giving satisfactions. At one moment they are rewards assessed and given for competence in skill and performance within the formalized activity, and at other times through the felt-joy or good feeling in a less formalized, more abstract and individualistic sense gained by participation, possibly in the same activity; where the activity, or any part of programme is being used by a number of people with different reward expectancies there is likely to be conflict. Those who wish to use the activity to gain satisfactions by reaching skill competence which can be measured, standardized or graded will challenge the use of the activity by those who are seeking different sorts of satisfactions. The resolving of the conflict is part of the education process and the youth worker needs to apply his group work skill in such situations, and the understanding of what activities *do* for individuals and *why* individuals are using them as vehicles for meeting their needs is a prerequisite to applying this skill.

Programme Analysis

At the beginning of this chapter we suggested that programme planning begins with identifying needs, recognizing that those needs can be satisfied in a variety of ways and that there are organizational limitations. Now we add another framework for the analysis of the effect of programme, which can be used to look at the total programme or parts of it. Everything that is done when the young people are in associations as members of the Club is programme. Clubs, like schools and similar institutions, have timetables, if not printed and pinned to notice boards there is a time-tabling sequence and sessional plan about each club meeting. Certain things dictate how this shall be done, such as, time for coming and going; space and its restrictions as well as its possibilities; staff and their availability as well as their skill; services such as coffee bar, refreshments, cleaning preparation and restoration of premises; use of outside facilities; seasonal requirements and implications, not only to do with seasonal activities like football, cricket and leagues and competitions but special events at Christmas, Easter, and other national occasions. Important as this is, and it does direct much of planning in imposing limitations as well as affording opportunities, there is much more 'free' time within the time-table not taken-up in the more formalized activity groupings, and all of this time is programme and how it is used and perceived by the members has to be taken into any analysis of programme effect.

1. *Participation:* Too often overlooked in programme planning is the basic question of who can participate and what are the criteria for participation. Adults will tend to have criteria based on their own ability to join organizations or activities and too seldom try to see this through the eyes of young people and what it takes or requires to be able to join an organization or activity. Unwittingly adults put up barriers. For instance, when a group of fifteen-year-olds sheltering in a shop doorway one cold and wet evening were asked if they had ever wanted to join the Youth Club over the way, they replied 'yes, but there's a notice

outside which says "No Visitors – Members Only".'

So the questions or considerations are:
(*a*) Who can participate?
(*b*) At what level can they participate – are there any membership restrictions such as 'temporary membership', 'probationary (what an unfortunate use of the word) membership', 'full membership'?
(*c*) Does a high minimum standard of competence prevent participation?
(*d*) Is there some system governing joining an activity which is obscure to newcomers but 'obvious' to regulars?
(*e*) How cohesive or closed are the groups? How does a person gain acceptance?
(*f*) What is the degree of commitment? Can a person float in and out of activity groups? What are the pressures on a person to make long-term choices, and who puts these pressures?

2. *Content:*
The particular agency will determine, to some degree, the content of the programme and the particular goals will have to be kept in mind when considering the general goals of youth work.
(*a*) Are there opportunities for providing satisfactions in skills as well as for social education?
(*b*) What governs popularity of an activity? Is it the opportunities it affords for large number participation and wider interaction: for freedom from controls imposed by the discipline of more formalized approaches?
(*c*) Does the programme contain activities which are just pastimes where it would be difficult, even if it was wise, to addanother 'effective' dimension to them, e.g. darts, football machines.
(*d*) What type of activity lends itself to centralizing power and control in the hands of a few or a single person? Where an adult is central to an activity, e.g. instructor, team manager, how does he release the members' dependence on him?

3. *Physical Considerations:* There are two parts to this (1) space available and how it is used (2) mobility within particular activities.

(*a*) How is space perceived – as directing what can be done and conditioning what it cannot be used for?

(*b*) Can atmosphere be created by skilful use of space and furnishing so that alternative ways of presenting the same activity produce other satisfactions? (When members complain about the sameness of programme or of boredom perhaps they are saying more about presentation than the worth of activity).

(*c*) What frustrations accrue from attempts to carry out an activity with inadequate space? What are the effects on behaviour when a compromise has to be made? Should these activities be pursued under such conditions? Can they be done elsewhere and will members go elsewhere to do them? If not, why not? (The answer to the last questions may give a clearer indication of what they expect from the programme.)

(2)(*a*) What does the activity require in bodily movement and how does this effect the behaviour of the participants?

(*b*) Which activities, conditioned by rules, restrict the number who can participate at any one time? (badminton, two or four players and a great deal of space, compared with touch-rugby for as many as wish, in the same space). Which activities offer opportunities for physical aggression and bodily contact, and which offer opportunities for physical exercise with no bodily contact (there may still be an aggression content)? These are usually team games as opposed to individual contests, football compared with tennis, but there are exceptions like cricket, boxing, wrestling. Judo is an example of 'controlled' aggression.

Co-operation

If one of the aims of the youth worker and the desire of the members is co-operation, then the programme has to be assessed in terms, not merely of co-ordination because that can be achieved by competent time-tabling, but in the quality of relationships, the 'good' feelings existing between all involved, the depth of involvement in the total programme and a growing awareness of the goals of the organization or club as understood by the agency and the youth worker. Again the youth worker can examine parts of his programme to gain insights into what this co-operation is and how it is achieved.

(*a*) Are there some activities which lend themselves to a need for a high degree of co-operation for their successful achievement? Why is this so? For example, a club camp, a concert, entertaining other groups, rambling, the Christmas party and a host of other activities require and afford opportunities for involvement by numerous people. Various levels of competence in a wide range of ability and knowledge are required; these are tasks which can be undertaken by people with little previous knowledge or special ability: individuals or small groups can have special responsibilities and be the 'expert(s)' in that area for this special event: none are seen as more important than the others for the whole is only as good as the parts: emphasis is on helping or facilitating each other for the sake of the desired success of the end product. The rewards are in the feelings of having played an important role in co-operation and in the final outcome of the event.

(*b*) How am I helping members to understand the whole as well as parts of it? Is there sufficient interaction between individuals and groups? How can this be increased through the groups and individuals becoming aware of the need to facilitate and help each other? Can experience where this has happened be analysed by the members, maybe with my help or is it enough to be satisfied that they have had the experience and hope that one day they will learn from it?

This chapter has attempted to bring some of the background knowledge of previous chapters to the task of planning and evaluating programme content. What it has not done is plan a programme or present a list of activities or give 'tips' of what can be successful, or disastrous, if included in any club programme. For someone like the author or anyone else in a training or helping role to tell a youth worker what he should put in the programme would be a denial of all that has been said or implied in this book. If one gains anything from experience it is the reasons *why* things have appeared acceptable to some young people and appeared to have met their needs and *not what* has been useful. There will be those who think that we are being too analytical about a simple thing like club work and others who will point out that young people's involvement in youth work is fleeting and, in any case, that things happen so spontaneously that the youth worker does not have time to stand back from the situation but has to act quickly. Whilst one sympathizes with the latter, it is because he has, so often, to act quickly that as many opportunities as possible should be taken to stand back from the immediate and day-to-day situation and apply some analytical processes to the job. In what other ways is he going to assess his effect, increase his knowledge and skills? To some degree he already does this as is demonstrated at weekend courses, leaders meetings, conferences and requests to youth officers and organizations for aid in a number of ways. What the approaches suggested here offer are ways of bringing more discipline to the thinking about the job in hand. It is this disciplined way of looking at what the youth worker is doing, the influence he has and how he uses it, by devising some framework he can use to guide his thinking, which will be the subject of the final chapter.

Chapter Nine

MANAGEMENT

In general, management is seen as an essentially practical activity. Management is both an art and a science based on personality and analysis, definition, orderliness and clarity of purpose and is part of the total skill of working with people. If there is a notion that concern for persons and management concerned with production can be separated in the industrial or commercial enterprise, it is certainly not possible in youth work. Management takes place within some structure or organization and an organization can be classified according to whether it is in being for production or to offer a service. Simpler, perhaps, to ask 'for whose benefit is the organization'? If it is a business concern its primary task may be to make a profit for the owners or shareholders and this is not to say that the customers do not gain from whatever is produced; it may be a public service like the Police Force or Fire Service in which case the organization benefits the public at large; or it may be a social service which is there to offer a service to individual clients with specific needs. An organization has an identity, it can be described and analysed and to some extent be consciously controlled so that it takes a form appropriate to given purposes. It should not be a static thing but malleable, not only capable of change but desiring to change according to needs. It is, therefore, an instrument used by the worker in attempting to reach objectives. The immediate question in youth work is which is the organization; is it the Youth Service, the National organization to which the unit may be affiliated, the local education authority's youth service, the local unit or a sponsoring body like the Church which sees the youth work as part of a total organization? It can, in fact, be all of these or any amalgam of them. The Youth Service can be seen as an organization in this sense because it has an identity, it is recognizable in its many forms by the people who use it and by the public at large; it has plans and policies for attempting to meet certain aims and goals; there is a structure and it allows for different approaches by groups of people or even individuals. This can be so for the National Organizations and the local education authorities. At unit level the only difference might be that this is *one particular approach* to meeting the aims and goals of the Youth Service.

Organizations tend to acquire needs of their own and produce rules and regulations which appear to come from people they serve or to promote some form of equality in the way needs are met, often under the cloak of being impartial, to the extent that they are unable to meet individual needs. Any individual who displays problems outside the 'norm' is seen as a threat or as different. Such rigidity in rules and regulations can also provide shelter for the worker who can justify not helping some persons by claiming to have to work within the agency rules or policy. Efficiency must be related to purpose and goals and not only in terms of orderliness and tidiness. Conversely, of course, untidiness and an unorderly state does not mean the purpose or desired ends for people using the agency is being met efficiently. At times orderliness and tidiness may have to give way to experiment, learning and individualism on the part of those using the service, but this should be a conscious decision on the part of the agency or worker and not an excuse for not caring. And such situations should be seen as opportunities for constructive movement towards the goals of the organization.

The organization is concerned with policy, with defining aims and objects and the provision of resources in order that those aims and objects may be achieved. The policy-making function needs to recognize that the resources it can call on depend largely on what society sanctions not only in the financial sense of paying for what it considers worthwhile but how far it will allow or tolerate the existence of such units and encourage young people to spend some of their leisure time 'under that sort of influence'. In some situations, recognizable to those who work in a number of Church clubs, there can be an immediate society of church members who doubt the value of club work (in relation to other forms of youth work within the Church) and make the obtaining of available resources difficult. The organization is effected by developments in other spheres and youth work has moved from a first-aid, rescue operation towards a more positive role of social education. Developments in medicine, schooling, housing, employment and the increased mobility and spending power of the young have meant that the policy-making function is a highly sophisticated one needing informed opinion, sensitivity to the needs of young people and some knowledge of different techniques in meeting those needs. Youth Service has been effected by developments in sociology, social psychology and the theories coming from group work and case practice. No unit of youth work can remain unaffected by other agencies at work in the immediate environment. Many of the other agencies, certainly those in the social work field, are formalized, in a sense, by legislation so that their function is clear and what their function is not is also clear. This may not be so in the case of the Youth Service and the agency needs to take care it does not overstep its function by taking on the functions of another agency, for example, by becoming a youth employment bureau or a treatment clinic for a number of mental or physical disorders. Administration, says Professor Simon, is the art of getting things done.[1] It is a method by which conscious attempt can be made to ensure that in every respect possible, an organization is geared effectively to the work it has to do. The average youth worker thinks of 'admin' as a chore. He may concede that it is a necessary one, but a chore nevertheless and usually associates it with paperwork, with returns, forms, reports and the requests to support this scheme or that event, all of them remote from the 'real' job of running the club night by night. But administration consists of everything to do with the policies of the organization whether this be the Youth Service at national level or at unit level. It is to do with policy-making, putting that policy into action and modifying it according to changing circumstances. The functions of administration are based on the concepts of leadership, decision-making, authority and communication. In all organizations someone is placed in the role of leader or head usually because he is seen as having certain skills and competence conducive to the task in hand. This person accepts the organization's policy and works towards the organization's goals. Part of his leadership function is to continually assess the work being done and circulate it in terms of the organization's aims. This will lead to demands for

[1] *Working with Administrations* (Case Conference, Feb. 1966).

resources, both manpower and material, to meet the needs of those who are to benefit from the organization. Part of this function may be to help the policy-making body redefine purpose in light of change. This person, accepting the role of leader, should feel it to be his responsibility for choosing certain lines of action within the limitations of the organization. Some of these limitations may mean that certain actions he would like to take are not possible. They may be to do with the numbers of young people he can accept into membership for reasons of safety or restrictions to do with age-range or Church membership. Other decisions may not be limited or described by the management or policy committee or by law but there will be an expectation that he will exercise integrity in choosing what can and cannot be done in the name of the Club or organization. For instance he will be responsible for the care of people in their use of the building, equipment and the programme. No matter what techniques he uses for the development of the work he must accept responsibility for what results from this and see himself as answerable to his agency. The leader may promote a high degree of self-programming by the members and believe that this is desirable to meet the aims of the agency but he must accept the risk involved. Over protection can limit this sort of growth; allowing the members full-rein may be very valuable in learning experiences but may have repercussions beyond the club programme and the membership. The leader must accept the responsibility for whatever arises from action because he has sanctioned the form of the action after thinking through how it will be used and what the possible implications will be. Some of these long-term decisions will be reached after consultation with other adult helpers, members and possibly, the policy or management committee. The leader and the others involved should see it as the leader's task to reach a decision as a result of consultation and not use consultation to impose a decision on the leader. Naturally the youth leader has to make night-by-night and almost minute-by-minute decisions in this relationship with members and staff and this is dealt with in the chapter on the youth worker's role.

Authority is inherent in the relationships between the adult and the members. It is an unavoidable part of the relationship where one person is in a position of responsibility and more so in a situation of caring for and helping other people. The task is one of tempering the authority the leader has with his desire to support the rights of those he serves to be self-determining. If this person is expected to make decisions then authority is seen as the power for reaching and carrying out decisions which effect the conduct or functioning of those using the organization whether as co-workers or clients. Here we are not using the word authority as a classification of a type of leader (types of leadership can be classified autocratic, authoritarian, democratic, laissez-faire).

Communication is the fourth function of the leader in his role of administrator. In any healthy organization lines of communication have to be established and methods of using them worked out. The usual notion of lines of communication in an organization are one going up giving information and one coming down giving decisions. It is unrealistic to think that these are the only lines of communication which exist or are desirable in an organization. Communication goes on laterally as well as vertically, certainly in the informal structure of the organization. In club work there is a tendency to channel opinion and information in straight vertical lines, that is, through the members' committee and activity groups to the leader or staff and to see opinion forming in the lateral and informal setting as irksome and rebellious. Members may be made to feel guilty if they do not use the 'proper' channels to communicate their feelings, when they may have little faith in the formal structure or, for a number of reasons, feel unable to use it. The task here is to recognize that people are none the less healthy or rebellious because they feel a need to communicate in this way, and then use this system of communication to promote efficiency rather than see it as a hindrance. There are four areas which need study in this context:

1. Member level. Examine the formal structure and the informal structure of the club or unit to discover the lines of communication which have been formally established and those which have developed outside it. What is the function of the parts of the formal structure, how are they used and to

what effect, for instance, how does one assess that the members' committee or similar representative group is representative, does speak for the majority, sub-groupings and individuals, expresses real feelings; how is information gathered and disseminated.

2. Staff level. How remote is the head or leader from the rest of the staff; what does he communicate to them and how does he do this; are some members of the staff more 'in the picture' than others; are there opportunities for staff sessions which enable people to express how they feel about their roles, to challenge policy and method.

3. Management Committee level. What is the leader's role here – is he seen as a person with some skill in putting policy into action; how does he communicate what is being achieved, what does the Committee want to know about his work, how does he evaluate what is being done; by what criteria does the leader view the committee as restrictive, helpful or merely a necessary, but irksome, part of the structure; are there parts of his work with young people he feels unable to discuss with the committee.

4. Organizational level where the club or unit is part of a larger body. This can be as part of a local education authority service and/or part of a national youth organization or Church. The leader may be one of a number of people employed or engaged by the organization and he will have communication with colleagues laterally as well as vertically in a hierarchical sense. In some situations, such as within the Church, community centre or school, he may have to work within another structure and learn how to use the lines of communication within this.

Administration should be seen as ways and means of ensuring that services are available to meet the needs of the young people using the club or unit. The leader's administrative task is to interpret these needs to those who control and provide the resources and make it possible for those who operate as members of staff (themselves part of the resources of the organization) to carry out work effectively. The three groups, the policy-making and resource providing group, the workers and the users of the service, that is, the members must be closely linked by lines of communication established and kept in use for the project to work in the direction of its purpose. The leader will be the vehicle for much of the communication but he should not be the only means and part of his responsibility is to encourage other means.

Areas of Management

The person in the role of manager or administrator must see accountability as a duty in all the areas of managing. He may see this accountability related to different groups of people, to the management or adult committee, the Church, a national organization, the local education authority, the young people, parents, staff, neighbours and the community. There are certain areas of management common to all who work at unit level irrespective of the nature of the organization or its purpose. These can be examined as follows:

1. *Records Related to Users of the Service.* Generally there is some requirement on the leader to record the number of young people using the club, unit or organization. This may be limited to how many are in association or extensive to include a great deal of information about each person. The leader needs to work out procedures which provide adequate information with the minimum amount of bookwork or use of staff time unless he sees the information being gathered through staff-member contacts when, possibly, other purposes are being achieved. In those youth work situations where some form of membership is part of the structure certain detail is required and may be recorded as soon as the young person applies for membership. This may be as simple as names, address and date of birth which are entered in a membership register, sometimes used for recording attendances and subscriptions. It would serve little purpose to try to enumerate – much less evaluate the different methods used to keep such records. The purpose of the organization, the expectations of parents and the community, the information required by sponsoring or supporting bodies may demand that the leaders keep records of membership and nightly attendances. The leader may see it as wise to keep

such records for safety or legal reasons and he may also believe it essential if he is to help each individual person because such recordings can give him useful information.

Such basic information should not be confused with other records he may wish to keep and which can be seen as professional or confidential records of individual members. So he needs to ask himself what is the basic information of a non-confidential nature which is available to any of the staff or members where they take part in registering attendances and collecting subscriptions and, if he needs to keep other records, what are they for, how and where are they kept and how confidential are they.

During recent years clubs have made it possible for visitors to use some of the club's resources and have a booking system of members' and 'visitors'. The latter can be almost as regular as the former but they usually pay different rates for entry on a night-by-night basis and are not entitled to the same rights as members (incidentally they do not have the corresponding duties). Where this happens the leader needs to have a system of 'booking in' or counting heads. In large membership clubs where there is a register of members and attendances there is a tendency to give each member a membership number. Recently, the author witnessed an adult helper registering members as they arrived and showing great ability in putting a number to a face. When asked how many names she could put to faces she admitted very few but with great pride said she knew at least 60 per cent by their numbers! Come in No. 51!

Registers and card-index systems can be purchased and adapted to youth club use. The adaptations will depend on the system required, of course, and where one needs to register attendances and can combine this with payment of subscriptions a great deal of time can be saved. Here are two examples:

	FEBRUARY																												
	1	2	3	4	5	6	7	8	9	10	11	12	13	14	15	16	17	18	19	20	21	22	23	24	25	26	27	28	*Arrears*
Adams, E.	√	√			√	5		√	√			√	√	5			√				√	5	√	√		√	5		NIL
Brown, J.		√		√	√				√		√	√		10		√	√			√	5		√	√		√	5		NIL
Brook, A.		√	√	√	√	5		√	√	√	√				√	√	√			√			√		√		10		5
Cook, S.		√		√		5		√							√							√					√		1

	JANUARY					FEBRUARY				
	W/E 7th	W/E 14th	W/E 21st	W/E 28th	*Arrears*	W/E 4th	W/E 11th	W/E 18th	W/E 25th	*Arrears*
Adams, E.	√ √ √ √ 5	√ √ √ 5	√ √ √ √ 5	√ √ √ 5	NIL					
Brown. S.	√ √ √	√ 5 √ √	√ 10 √ √	√ 5 √ √	NIL					
Brook, A.	√ √ √ √	√ √ √	√ 10 √	√ 5 √ √	5					
Cook, S.	√ √	√ √	√ √	√ √ 5	15					

In both cases arrears of subscription is totalled and entered at the end of each month, but this assumes that there is a ruling that a weekly subscription is paid rather than the nightly subscription. With the latter system if subscription or entry fees are registered, naturally, that also shows attendance.

2. *Finance*

The leader will be involved in money transactions almost daily. Some of the responsibility may be taken from him by a club treasurer, members of staff or adult committee but he will still be accountable for a great deal of the actual cash and certainly for those goods purchased with it whether he actually handles the money or not. Money will come to him through members' subscriptions, canteen or coffee bar takings, payments for courses, holidays, purchases of club equipment, donations, grants, collections, special money-raising events, and so on. As money is received it should be recorded and banked and as many payments as possible made by cheque from the club account. Only those incidental, small, day-to-day expenses should be paid by cash through the petty cash account – this is originally a cheque payment and should not be supplemented by takings.

Petty Cash Account. No matter what size the undertaking the leader needs to have a sum of money in hand for small payments. He obtains this by having a cheque drawn on the club account for a sum which it is estimated will meet the demand of small payments for, say one month. Having cashed the cheque he will use this money, getting receipts for expenditure, until he requests that the sum is made up to the original amount. This is done by presenting the receipts for money spent together with a statement of cash in hand. A cheque for the amount spent should then be made out which added to the cash in hand comes to the original petty cash amount. The example of the Petty Cash Book (Figure V) shows the amount as £10 and on 21st October it was made up to this sum by cashing a cheque for £9·63. The expenditure over the next four days was £8·29 and another cheque had to be drawn for this amount to make up the original £10. Either the sum of £10 is inadequate to meet the petty cash requirements or the milk and minerals accounts should be settled by cheque from the main club account. Where the leader is unable to get receipts, for instance for bus fares, he makes out a petty cash voucher (these can be purchased from a stationer) and gets a signature. This petty cash book itemizes the purchases for easy transfer to the club accounts book.

Income and Expenditure Account. Obviously there is a need for recording money coming in and money being paid out by the organization. This is recorded in the Cashbook or Income and Expenditure Ledger (Figure VI), usually itemized, according to the nature of the concern and the frequency of money coming in and going out under the various headings, for easier analysis. Such a cashbook or accounts ledger shows all money transactions whether paid or received as bank cheques or loose cash. Entries should be as explanatory as possible and entered against the date received. The petty cash items are transferred to this book when that account is made up to its original amount (compare the itemized entry for 25th October in the expenditure ledger with the example of the petty cash book). Money should be paid into the club's account as often as possible and not held in hand. The money received by the leader through cash transactions should be recorded as received and the full amount passed through this account, that is, into the bank, and no part of it used to pay bills or make up the petty cash.

Receipts should be given for money received and accounts from traders numbered, retained and filed in number order as a record of payment and a check on the accounting system. Clubs having accounts with traders will receive statements from them showing the state of their trading account. These are statements similar to the club's bank statements and should not be seen as accounts requesting payment.

The petty cash book and the income and expenditure ledger(s) are the main financial records common to all clubs and organizations, but the leader may be expected to keep other records such as a postage book recording to whom letters, circulars or packages are sent and at what cost: a telephone calls book recording calls, duration of time, cost of the call and whether private or business: canteen stock and account book separate to the income and expenditure ledgers to show balance between purchases, sales and stock in hand, and to assess the 'run' on certain lines. At certain times other financial records may be required distinct from the normal income and expenditure account, for instance, a club holiday fund or some special money-making effort undertaken by the members on behalf of some 'cause'. All of these should be seen as showing more detail but not necessarily as separate bank accounts and it is prudent to pass the monies involved through the one club account.

The leader should see it as a duty to try and obtain the best services for money expended. He owes this both to his clients and his organization. In this respect he needs to negotiate with traders for the best terms and to seek tenders for certain items of equipment or consumable goods and for the best follow-up service, such as delivery, maintenance of equipment, guarantees of service, rates of discount for quantity or early payment of accounts. Some of these services he will obtain through personal contact or through the sympathy of the trader for the work he is doing, but as a general rule he should want to establish this in a business-like manner. Ordering services should not be by personal contact only but followed up by a business-like practice. This means giving an order in writing, preferably on an order form, stating clearly the requirement, the cost quoted by the trader and the delivery date. The leader's responsibility extends then to seeing that the order is carried out, checked to his satisfaction, acknowledged to the trader and recorded for his organization and, subsequently, the account checked against the order and delivery and paid as soon as possible.

3. *Buildings and Equipment*. Youth clubs and organizations meet in a wide variety of buildings and few of them are totally

Figure V –Petty Cash Book

Receipts			Payments									
Date	Cheque No:	Amount	Date	Item	Voucher No:	Total	Cleaning Materials	Repairs	Small Equipment	Canteen	Postage	Sundry Expenses
B/f		0·37	22 Oct.	Milk	044	2·13				2·13		
21 Oct.	420	9·63	23 Oct.	Table Tennis Balls	045	0·60			0·60			
				Glass & Putty	046	0·47		0·47				
			24 Oct.	Newspapers, Mags.	047	0·75						0·75
				Pins, Clips	048	0·21			0·21			
			25 Oct.	Fares	049	0·28						0·28
				Minerals	050	3·05				3·05		
				Postage	051	0·63					0·63	
				Pencils, String	052	0·17						0·17
		10·00			Total:	8·29		0·47	0·81	5·18	0·63	1·20
					Balance in hand C/d.	1·71						
						10·00						
C/f.		1·71	29 Oct.	Soap powder etc.	053	0·78	0·78					
25 Oct.	425	8·29										

Figure VI – Cash Book

	Item	Receipt No.	Total	Paid to Bank	Subs.	Canteen	Donations	Grants	Holiday Fund	Sale of Badges, Crafts	Special Events	Other Receipts
	B/forward		188·73	188·7	30·20	48·24	7·35	100·00		0·37		2·57
23 Oct.	Camford County Borough	249	34·00					34·00				
	M/s. Joules Ltd.	250	2·10				2·10					
24 Oct.	Collections for Old People's Fund	251	1·98									1·98
26 Oct.	Club takings W/E 26 Oct.	(252)	29·99		6·60	12·17			10·50	0·72		
26 Oct.	Club Dance		48·17			7·17					41·00	

Date	Item	Voucher or Cheque No.	Total	Lighting Heating Cleaning	Rent Rates Insurance	Repairs Renewals	Holidays	Course Fees	Activity Equipmt.	Canteen	Stationery Postage	Wages Insur-ance	Sundries
	B/forward		89·31		4·50	3·07		1·13		25·04	4·05	46·05	5·47
23 Oct.	S. Elec. Board	421	10·11	10·11									
	Smith & Jones	422	5·63							5·63			
24 Oct.	Inter Global Travelling Co.	423	30·00				30 0 0						
	Sportings Ltd.	424	42·00						42·00				
25 Oct.	Petty Cash	425	8·29			0·47			0·81	5·18	0·63		1·20
29 Oct.	M. J. Spark Co. Ltd.	426	2·24			2·24							
	Dress-U-Up Ltd.	427	1·13						1·13				

responsible for their own premises. Far more meet in premises which were built and are used for other purposes. In either case the leader needs to understand the limitations imposed by the building and the expectations of other groups of people as to how they see the building being used. Accepting the limitations, his task may be twofold. The first is to minimize the limitations by improvisation and obtaining the co-operation of his staff and members so that the best possible atmosphere and programme can be reached. The limitations imposed where there is dual use of premises can be used as an excuse for not using one's imagination. Worse, perhaps, is not seeing it as a challenge to young people's imagination and creativity. Secondly, the leader needs to find ways of negotiating with the other users for the improvement of conditions to their mutual advantage.

4. *The Management or Sponsoring Body*. The leader is normally responsible to some form of adult management or sponsorship for maintaining an on-going concern, to carry out a policy within certain procedures or methods of work and such a body has a duty to see that the leader has the resources necessary for the work to be done. This implies some form of regular and systematic communication between the two. The leader's task is to acquaint the sponsoring body with facts about the young people using the service offered, some evaluation of the benefit they are deriving through their membership, the state of the resources available and developments in the way the work is being done. The management committee's task is to afford the opportunities for the leader, and his staff, to present their thoughts on progress and to discuss ways in which the requests or needs of the members and staff can be met. This body will rely on the leader, as the practitioner, for a demonstration of his understanding of young people's needs, the techniques employed to gain this understanding and his skill in using this within the general aim of the organization. It will also expect him to know how to use the lines of communication to other agencies, such as the local education authority in order to obtain benefit from the services it offers, and to inform them of trends and current thinking about youth work in the more general sense.

This suggests that the business arises from the work the leader is doing and he needs to be involved in all deliberations and proposed action because his expertise is valued. His duty is to be business-like in the presentation of his report. The leader's report to the management body could follow this outline:

(*a*) the present position in regard to membership with a breakdown into age groups, male and female, school and work; staff, showing evenings on duty, function; premises and equipment – use and state. The leader might wish to make comparison with figures shown in his previous report.

(*b*) group life of the club; commenting on the sub-groupings, activity, corporate action, morale, self-government.

(*c*) planning for the future, the shape of the programme, meeting needs of different groupings of young people.

(*d*) relationships within the community, the club in relation to the local youth service, the Church, other social services, the immediate neighbourhood.

(*e*) requests to the management committee for:
  (i) more resources.
  (ii) approval to pursue special activities.
  (iii) reconsideration of policy.

(*f*) comments on documents relating to the Youth Service which are likely to reach the leader but not necessarily the members of the committee.

(*g*) a financial statement.

Such a report should be well prepared and presented, and preferably be in the hands of the committee before the meeting. If the report cannot be circulated to all before the meeting it is courteous and prudent to discuss it with the chairman before the meeting. Care should be taken in the use of jargon, or youth work language, in the report. Weaknesses should not be glossed over and the leader should attempt to present honest comments and not become sentimental.

5. *Publicity and Public Relations*

From time to time the leader will see it as desirable to demonstrate work being done by his organization in order, at least, to keep in front of the general public the fact that the organization exists. It is difficult to convey to the public the real worth of youth work in terms of human happiness and individual growth. Demonstrations need to be specific practical functions and are often viewed suspiciously as 'window dressing', more by those working in the youth service at grass roots level than by parents and the public at large. Special events like presentations of plays, concerts, athletic displays, public speaking competitions may require extra effort on the part of leaders to persuade members to participate and may not reflect what the club is offering or achieving with the majority but it may be essential to do this in order to maintain a favourable public image. It may well be an assumption that the general public will think it reflects what the club is doing week-by-week as it may be an assumption that they think club work is all table tennis and dancing. These and other publicity events, such as 'open-house', parents evenings, acts of service, can of course give a great deal of pleasure to both the givers and receivers. Seeking publicity through the Press creates some problems for the youth leader and at times he gets publicity he does not seek. The local Press is generally seen as favourable to such organizations and is often prepared to print statements on current or proposed events or stories about some 'unusual' happening. Invitations to special events, whether for the general public or for members only, are usually accepted and reported. Perhaps the greatest care has to be taken in making verbal statements, particularly where one may be critical of other organizations or groups of people, and finding these in print but not all the other comments made at the same time. But good public relations or a good public image does not depend only on the special events and the Press. Much more depends on the relationships between the different users of the same premises, the treatment of property and neighbours, the honouring of commitments, offering service to individuals and other organizations, dealings with trades people and the conduct of members in a whole range of situations some not within the club programme.

Chapter Ten

The Legal Position of the youth leader

No matter how arbitrarily we may have defined 'young people' in the past, it is now a fact in law that the age of majority is reached at eighteen (1968). Perhaps it is equally important for the youth worker to recognize the social and technical significances of this. 'The young, and all the sensible people connected with them, find it quite ludicrous that legally speaking a married man with three children and a car can be referred to as an "infant". Of all our conclusions the easiest we have found to arrive at is that this word should no longer be used and that the word "minor" should instead be substituted for those under the age of majority.'[1] The Report of the Committee on the Age of Majority pointed out that they were influenced in their recommendation that the age of majority be reduced from 21 to 18 by the evidence that 'the vast majority of young people are in fact running their own lives, making their own decisions and behaving as responsible adults by the time they are eighteen' and that 'there is undeniably a great increase in maturity towards that age' (page 39). The Latey Committee took note of those witnesses, 'who seemed most closely in touch with the young', favouring eighteen as the age when it was advisable to give responsibility and, possibly, undesirable to withhold it from persons, who themselves reckoned they were of age for such adult status and responsibility. There may well have been more faith than empirical evidence to support the statements 'that an important factor in coming of age is the *conviction* that you are now on your own' and 'given responsibility at 18, they would rise to the occasion'. But as the Report pointed out there is sufficient legislation to protect those who may not be able to 'rise to all occasions' and may find it difficult to resist the influence and powers of persuasion of people who wish to

[1] *Report of the Committee on the age of Majority* (the Latey Report) H.M.S.O. (page 42).

make capital out of the lack of experience of the young.

The significant technical factors in the lowering of the age of majority to 18[1] are that, at that age, young people are free to make binding contracts, marry, without first obtaining the consent of their parents or the court: are not liable to be made wards of court and are free to own and dispose of property. In other fields the law makes special terms for young people, for instance, serving on a jury and taking public office is still not attainable until age 21. The social implication of the lowering of the age of majority has effect on how we refer to young people in such institutions as colleges, the youth service, the youth and community field. In such institutions they may resent the umbrella terms like youth, immature teenagers, and, whilst sharing some of the uncertainties, misapprehensions and lack of experiences with those under eighteen, may demand a different approach because socially and legally they feel able to be classed as adult. In this chapter we examine the law as it affects the youth worker in relation to his clients, others using the premises and the use to which the premises can be put.

The legal position of the youth leader in respect of the young people in his care is not dependent on the payment to him of a salary, or the source of any salary paid. It falls to be determined in accordance with the general principles of the *law of tort*. A tort has been defined as 'the breach of a duty primarily fixed by the law, where the duty is one towards persons generally and its breach is redressable by an action for damages'. Whilst it might be thought desirable in principle that there is one single overriding duty imposed by law on all of us not to damage or injure our neighbours' interests without legal justification, it is preferable to regard the law of tort as a list of specific wrongs and remedies. It is impossible in such a book as this to discuss all torts and, in the main, we are concerned with those which affect the person rather than people's property. The main area of concern will be with the tort of negligence which has been defined by Baron Alderson in *Blyth* v. *Birmingham Waterworks Co.* as follows: 'Negligence is the omission to do something which a reasonable man, guided upon those considerations which ordinarily regulate the conduct of human affairs, would

[1] *Family Law Reform Act 1969*: H.M.S.O.

do, or doing something which a prudent or reasonable man would not do.'

Unlike the teacher, for example, there is virtually no legal history concerning the legal liability of the youth leader for his members. However, he will owe the ordinary duty of care in negligence to his membership as to any other person whom he can reasonably foresee might be injured by his acts or omissions. The degree of care required by the law will depend on the particular circumstances of each case, although, as a general principle the degree of care which must be exercised where children are concerned is greater than that required in respect of adults, and the age, maturity and character of the child would be important considerations. Because the nature of youth and community work involves work with children, adolescents and adults there is need to consider all these categories.

Parent and Child

It is a general principle of the law that the duty of care to be exercised by a person in charge of children includes the duty to exercise such supervision over the children in his care as to prevent as far as is reasonably possible, injury being caused to one child, by the act or omission of another. Any breach of this duty resulting in injury would give cause for action by the injured person. The degree of care to be exercised is a question of fact in each case, and the age and character of the child would be important factors, but the standard care is higher where children are likely to be affected by an adult's conduct. Examples from the courts help to illustrate these points. In a Canadian case, *Yachuk* v. *Oliver Blais Co.*, where two boys in their early teens persuaded a garage attendant to let them have a tin of petrol on the grounds that their mother's car had run out of petrol then poured it over some timber and set light to it, and the explosion of the petrol vapour caused the boys serious injuries, the Judicial Committee of the Privy Council held that the garage attendant had been negligent in entrusting the children with a dangerous commodity, namely, petrol. Where a boy of 15 shot the plaintiff with an air gun, it was held that the defendant's father was liable as he knew the boy was of such disposition as not to be trusted with a gun and, therefore, the father was negligent (*Court* v. *Wyatt*, 1960). On the other hand, a father who allowed his son, aged 13, to have an air rifle on condition that he did not use it outside the house, and had a large cellar in which the rifle could be used, was held not liable when, in disobedience to his orders, his son fired the rifle in an alleyway and injured a boy aged 15. The precautions taken were held as suitable and would have been adequate but for the son's disobedience (*Donaldson* v. *McNiven*, 1952).

Teacher and Pupil

It is accepted that the duty of the teacher is to take such care of his pupils as would a careful father of his children. This includes the duty to exercise supervision when children are in his care and the duty to ascertain that things such as tools, apparatus, etc., are not left lying about where they may be used by one child to cause injury to another. The amount of supervision required depends on the age of the pupils and what they are doing at the material time. During hours of instruction a greater degree of supervision is required than during hours of recreation. 'Encouragement of sturdy independence and the ability to get on without detailed supervision must start at an early age' (*per McNair J.* in *Jeffrey* v. *L.C.C.*). What things left lying about are likely to cause injury depends on the nature of the thing and the age of the pupils. 'To leave a knife about where a child of 4 could get at it would amount to negligence but it would not if boys of 18 had access to it' (*per Cave J.* in *Williams* v. *Eady*, 1893).

If a teacher knows, or ought to know, that the pupils on school premises are playing games in such a manner or place as to be likely to cause injury to themselves, he is negligent if he does not take proper steps to prevent the danger. When the plaintiff, one of several children playing 'touch' in classroom with a glass partition, put his hand through the glass, it was held that the defendants were liable, as a reasonably prudent parent would have contemplated the danger (*Ralph* v. *L.C.C.*, 1947). When a schoolboy aged 16 was injured by an air pistol discharged by a fellow pupil during an unsupervised period at school, it was held that the school was not liable, as it would be too onerous to require that a class of twenty aged about 16 years should be constantly supervised (*Harris* v. *Guest*, 1960).

Youth Leader and Members

As stated above there is little legal history concerning the liability of the youth leader for the activities of his members. There can be little doubt, however, that the general principle enunciated above would apply and that the application of this principle to the cases quoted would be a good guide to its application in the case of the youth leader and his member. There are certain factors which the courts might give particular attention to when considering the liability of the youth leader for the activities undertaken by the members of his club:

1. the youth leader is not in *loco parentis* in the same sense as the school teacher. Membership of a youth club is voluntary and the courts would see the club leaders' degree of authority and amount of control as less than that of the school teacher;
2. it might well be considered that one of the major purposes of a youth club is to develop and encourage a sense of responsibility in its members with an expectation that they may pursue many of their activities with a minimum of supervision;
3. the members will normally be of an age at which they may reasonably be expected to think before they act.

The youth leader will still feel he owes a duty of care for all those people whom he may foresee as being in danger of injury if he should not act as a reasonable person would have done. Reasonable care will be exercised in respect of the safety of equipment and premises, including fire precautions and the posting of notices regarding action in the event of fire (one wonders how many clubs carry out fire drill). Safeguards in respect of certain hazardous activities including competent instruction and general insurance as well as extra insurance cover for special events and activities not normally covered in a general insurance policy.

Responsibility for Staff and Occupiers' Liability

The youth leader has a responsibility in law for any tort committed by a member of his staff or club member where he has made that person his servant or agent for a certain purpose and the tort is committed during the course of his employment or within the scope of his authority. He also owes the common duty of care to all visitors, that is, to take such care as in all the circumstances of the case is reasonable, to see that the visitor will be reasonably safe in using the premises for the purposes which he is invited or permitted by the occupier to be there (*Occupiers' Liability Act 1957*). The duty relates to the activities carried out on the premises as well as to the condition of the premises, by a third party who is not the servant or agent of the occupier. This means that if the club leader is termed the occupier because he is the person in control of the premises, as for example, a full-time leader or warden but this could include the voluntary leader working in a special building earmarked for youth activities, he could be liable where an injury is caused to one person by the activity of another, whether he (the leader) is present or not, because he has sanctioned the use of the premises.

Those entitled to the rights of visitors extends to persons who are on the premises to carry out such duties as reading meters, carrying out repairs, cleaning windows as well as to persons who enter the premises in the exercise of a right conferred by law. The occupier has no such obligation in respect of trespassers, that is, those who use the premises without permission or who continue to use the premises after permission has been withdrawn.

The Expectations of Society

In law a young person having left school or entered his teens is seen as largely responsible for his own actions, although particular factors such as age, degree of maturity, intelligence, character and cultural background will play a part in determining the level of responsibility and the youth leader is not seen as being in *loco parentis*. In general, then, this condition favours the youth leader in his task of helping young people to equip themselves to lead satisfying lives. But it is unreasonable to assume that parents of members and other adults in the close community understand or know this. It is also unreasonable to assume that all young people are as near to exercising responsibility as envisaged by the law. Many parents and other adults concerned see the leader as an extension of their adult authority and he will be identified with 'sound' mores of behaviour, law abiding and stable behaviour in a whole range of relationships and human activity. It may be a very high and unrealistic expectation but the leader needs to be aware of it. As with any professional worker or person holding office in the Church the youth leader comes under a level of public scrutiny higher than that usually levelled at the average citizen. His desire to accept all people and his methods of working in helping young people to an understanding and practice of self-determination may be misunderstood by parents and seen as a prime force in undermining their authority and standards. They may become concerned at the freedom offered to their children in an atmosphere of self-programming and consider not enough guidance and control comes from the club and the leader.

The leader needs to go beyond the interpretation of his duty in law for the sake of his members parents and other adults. This requires an ability to define his role and function and to take into his understanding the feelings of adult groups in the community about his work with young people. Failure to do this may result in adults withdrawing their support, forbidding their children to associate with the club and, probably worse, losing the opportunity to involve people, young and adult, in a corporate effort for the betterment of the community.

The responsibility of the leader extends beyond the club base and in one sense, where members are involved in activity as part of their club experiences but in places other than their club building, the leader will accept the same responsibility as for groups operating in the club building. But in another sense the leader may be seen as responsible for the behaviour of his members when, legally, he could argue that he has no responsibility. Nevertheless he needs to recognize that socially he will be identified with members' behaviour particularly immediately before and after club hours or when they use the immediate vicinity of the club for 'meeting-up' although there is no club meeting that night. The most common cause of complaint by the public, in this respect, is that of nuisance caused by obstruction, noise, illegal parking, minor and noisy affrays, trespass and interference with public facilities, for example, bus shelters, telephone kiosks, public lavatories, etc. The leader does not help the situation by refuting complaints from neighbours or passers-by. He does a disservice to both the complainant and the young people by ignoring the complaint or dismissing it in defence of young people. How he handles the situation depends on many factors but he should consider it his duty as a citizen as well as a youth leader to uphold the rights of the complainant and to help the young people to see why a complaint is being made. Beyond this he may feel he wants to inform the young people of the possible consequences, in law, if and when such complaints are made and his position in relation to them and the complainant.

The Legal Liability of Children

As a guiding principle it is wise to remember that in law a minor, that is, a person under eighteen is not liable upon his contracts. This does not include any of the acceptable, simple and commonplace contracts of everyday, such as, paying for services necessary or required at that moment, or in respect of indentures concerned with apprenticeships, or being an articled pupil. This is not likely to concern the youth leader in his day-to-day business transactions with members but where he may be organizing events such as holidays requiring members to pay large sums of money he would be wise to draw up some form of agreement which is guaranteed by the member's parent or guardian. Such an agreement could carry some form of indemnity whilst stating that the leader, acting on behalf of his employing agency, would take certain precautions to safeguard the participants and these would vary according to the nature of the exercise.

Use of Premises

Some of the limitations on the use of premises will evolve from the very nature of the agency and how it views certain activities. Any group using Church premises will be directed in what it can and cannot do on those premises as much by Church Law as Civil Law. Church Law may decree that there shall be no alcohol consumed on or taken into the buildings, no public dancing or gambling of any form even if licences could be obtained through the civil licensing authorities for such activity. The Club Leader and his management committee need to be conversant with Church Law, where this is applicable because the club is housed on church property, as well as with the civil laws and bye-laws which control such activities.

Licences are required in respect of a number of what have become normal club activities, some of which are issued by the local authority, being the licencing authority, and, others by associations protecting the interests of the association and its members. It may be useful to list a number of these, but such a list should not be seen as all-inclusive and where a youth worker has doubts about the legality of activity included in the programme he should seek further advice of the local authority.

Music, Singing and Dancing Licences are required for public performances and are issued by the local authority. Such licences indicate the maximum number of persons that can be admitted to the premises and prescribes the fire precautions to be taken.

Performing Rights A licence is required in respect of all musical works, whether published or in manuscript performed vocally, instrumental or mechanically at the premises. The licence is obtained from the Performing Right Society Ltd., who require that a list of all works performed, with names of Composer, Arranger and Publisher, and the number of times each has been performed. This may be for one occasion, such as a dance or musical evening, or over a period of time where music is being reproduced for use by members of the club. No such return is required in respect of radio and/or television programmes, the public performance of which may be covered by the licence.

Tape-recording and Copyright Prior permissionmust be obtained from the B.B.C. or I.T.V. for the making of a tape-recording of any sound broadcast or of the sound part of a television broadcast other than for private purposes. Permission must also be sought of the owners of the particular work's copyright before such recordings are used in public. Gramophone records should not be re-recorded on to a tape, whether for private or public purposes, this infringes the copyright of the record.[1]

Film Shows Clubs do not need a licence for showing films to members (the club needs to be a membership-club and not an organization which caters for 'clients' who need not be in membership). But if the club desires to give public film shows,

[1] *The Law and Your Tape-recorder*: A. Phelan: Print and Press Services (pamphlet 24 pages).

or invites non-members to film shows, then the Cinematograph Acts of 1909 and 1952 require that the club has a licence, issued by the local licensing authority. In this case conditions regarding children being admitted, number of attendants required, safety precautions are laid down by the licensing authority.

Lotteries or Gaming Lotteries are of three kinds or classifications.

(*a*) Small lotteries incidental to certain entertainments, such as bazaars, sales of work, fêtes, dinners, dances, sporting and other functions of a similar character. Prizes must not be money prizes and the whole proceeds of the entertainment, including the proceeds of the lottery, subject to certain deductions, must be devoted to purposes other than private gain. The sale and issue of tickets must take place on the premises where the entertainment takes place and during its progress, and there must be other inducements to persons to attend the entertainment other than the facility to take part in the lottery.

(*b*) Private lotteries where the sale of tickets or chances are confined to members of one society established and conducted for purposes not connected with gaming, betting or lotteries: persons working in the same establishment: or persons who live on the same premises.

(*c*) Lotteries promoted by societies registered with the local authority to raise money for their own purposes, such as, charitable purposes, support of athletic sports or games, or cultural activities, or other purposes not being for private gain or purpose of any commercial undertaking.

Games which form sideshows at a bazaar, sale of work, fête, dinner, dance, sporting event are legal so long as the whole proceeds of the event, including the proceeds of the game or amusement, are devoted to purposes other than private gain and that the opportunity to win a prize or to participate is not the only inducement to attend the event.

Gaming, including bingo, whist-drives, bridge, referred to as small gaming parties at entertainments promoted for raising money for purposes other than private gain are similarly controlled. In addition entrance fees or stakes are limited to 50p and there must be only one distribution of prizes, limited to £50 total value.[1]

Use of Boats, Canoes or Similar Craft Licences are required to make use of craft on most rivers and inland waterways, issued by the appropriate authority, such as a Conservancy Board or the Inland Waterways.

Public Service Vehicle Licence The Road Traffic Act, 1960, lays down special provisions for the licensing of motor vehicles used to carry passengers for *hire or reward.* Hire or reward is defined as any payment or consideration given by or on behalf of or received from a passenger, and any payment made to a club or society which entitles the passenger to be carried in one of its own vehicles also constitutes hire or reward even though the payment is not directly related to the journey or journeys made. Vehicles adapted to carry less than 8 passengers are not classed as Public Service Vehicles unless passengers are carried at *separate fares.* The expression separate fares covers not only what are generally understood as such, i.e. the case where separate payments are made by individual passengers directly to the operator, it covers arrangements in which separate payments for the journey are made whether these payments are made to the owner of the vehicle or to any other person. It is also immaterial whether the payments are made solely in respect of the journey or not.

Vehicles adapted to carry more than 8 passengers are classed as Public Service Vehicles and a correct P.S.V. licence is required: the driver must be over 21 years of age, holding a special licence entitling him to drive such a vehicle. Appropriate insurance cover in respect of passengers must be taken out.[2]

[1] *Voluntary Organizations and the Law relating to Lotteries and Gaming*: (pamphlet – 15 pages) published by the National Council of Social Service.

[2] A memorandum for guidance, PSV/A, can be obtained from the Regional Traffic Commissioners office.

Chapter Eleven

Towards a Disciplined Approach

Chapter Eight suggests that offering a programme of activities alone is not sufficient to satisfy the needs of people meeting in leisure time – recreational groups like youth clubs and organizations. There has been a growing realization that the social relationships which are created and used in a group are as important to the individuals as the activity. It has also been suggested that whatever the activity or stated reason for participation in it there are other processes going on in the group based on people's un-stated reasons for taking part in the activity. Most organizations as they have developed, have placed increasing emphasis on the need for opportunities for young people to gain social skills which appear to be neglected by other agencies, part of whose task it is to help in the maturing process. Further to this the social educator is concerned with individual persons rather than collections of people. He is concerned with the whole person, not merely with part of him as scholar, worker, or member, and how his various group-experiences influence his behaviour. The outcome of this is not what part the person plays in the success of a group project but how this relates to his full-life situation. This requires a professional approach to the work whether the worker is employed full-time or part-time and the key factor in a professional approach is discipline. How, then, can the youth worker no matter how employed or by whom bring a more disciplined approach to his work. There must be an assumption that he desires to help the people he serves make the most of all the experiences they have whilst members of the organization and influenced by his 'leadership'. Now he needs a framework of reference for disciplined thinking about his work and it is against this framework that he reflects on any part or all of the work he does within his task as youth worker. Such a framework may be in the form of general statements or questions such as:

1. What is the purpose of youth work and this particular agency or unit? The youth worker will continually ask himself 'am I pursuing the purpose of youth work and of my agency' in relation to his work with individuals and groups.

2. In what way does the agency see the unit functioning in order that the aims and purpose are met?

3. Who are the people who use this service? How much do I know about them? What are their expectations of the organization and me, and what are mine of them?

4. What are the limitations of the agency or unit? How are these viewed and handled by the members? How do I communicate to the members the limitations and the areas of freedom?

5. How do my reactions influence individuals and groups? Am I sensitive and perceptive about the inter-actions and inter-relationships in the unit?

6. What are the ethical concepts which guide me? These may be simply expressed as acceptance, a non-judgemental approach, desiring self-determination for individuals and groups, and confidentiality.

Recording

The youth worker has a responsibility to his agency for a variety of records and reports. These may include detailed membership lists, enrolments, subscriptions, minutes of meetings, financial statements and the like all of which may be useful to the worker and his agency in planning future action, budgeting and in evaluating programme effectiveness. But there is another type of recording which 'is becoming an integral part of social group practice rather than something separate and distinct from it. It is a tool for the improvement of group work and it has important values for the group, the worker, the agency and the field . . . such records help the worker to do a more effective job with his groups.'[1] Davies and Gibson make a further claim for the need of the social educator to use some tool which will aid his reflection because 'Social education, by its very nature, may require an adult to act spontaneously without

[1] *Social Group Work*: Harleigh B. Trecker: Association Press, New York 1955.

opportunity for lengthy reflection, and yet it is important that he avails himself as often as possible for the sources of guidance and illumination which are embodied in his purpose, principles and understanding.'[1] Recording as an aid to reflection with the objective of improving the youth worker's knowledge, self-awareness and application of his skill is a more disciplined and objective approach than the generalized, unscientific, spasmodic, descriptive, and often emotive, expressions of the progress of individuals, groups and the worker's role. When this is coupled with the further aid of supervision the worker is enabled to reach a higher standard in evaluating his work.

There are a number of barriers which have to be removed before one sets about developing a skill in recording. The first of these is the time factor, both to do with when one writes-up the recording and the amount of time and effort involved. The part-time worker feels this most strongly but it is not uncommon amongst full-time workers. If time is to be spent doing this then it has to be justified. The second barrier is the suspicion that it will not necessarily help the worker to do the job he is doing more effectively because recording, reflection and supervision do not produce answers or prescriptions. Another barrier may be the lack of someone skilled enough to help the youth worker to develop his recording, sharpen his reflective process and stimulate him to new understanding. Perhaps the resistance to recording as 'a new-fangled idea' as far as its application to youth work is concerned is less of a barrier now than it was a decade ago. There are a number of suggestions which may help the person who is about to learn how to record. Basically the art of recording is being able to commit to paper what the youth worker has observed, being able to analyse what this means, understanding what is going on in groups and what the interactions tell him about individuals. From this he needs to know what 'action' he has to take. Observing in this context is more than seeing, it means being receptive to all that is happening in the group situation. Hearing, sensing or feeling are as important as seeing. To observe does not necessarily mean standing back and watching, although from time to time this will happen, but being involved and participating in the group's affairs. The

[1] *Social Education of the Adolescent*: Davies and Gibson: U.L.P.

worker's powers of observation and perception can be developed through practice but only if he 'tests' them by some form of committing thoughts to words on tape or paper and checks what he has said or written with such questions as 'Is that what really happened?' 'How far does my previous knowledge and experience of this person, or persons, influence me – am I reading into the situation what I expected or did it really happen like that?' 'Can I be sure that I saw all, or heard all, or sensed all that was going on during that time?' 'In transmitting what was happening to memory and then to the written words what have I omitted, added, ignored, emphasized – and why?' 'Why have I selected this (or these) particular situations to write about and reflect on!' In a typical youth club the diversity of activity and of groups makes it impossible for the worker to record on everything for much of the inter-action is going on outside his sphere of observation and involvement. But he needs to be wary of not recording because 'nothing much happened'; there is always something happening which can deepen insights into human behaviour and, whilst it is attractive to record the dramatic or unusual incidents, we learn most about people in terms of their satisfactions, dissatisfactions, attitudes, likes and dislikes, aspirations and frustrations through the 'normal' and undramatic group experiences.

Factual Accounts – Narrative-type Recording

The worker has to learn how to record, how to transfer thoughts into symbols, either words on tape or, more commonly, as writing on paper, and at first he needs to do this to test the clarity and validity of his observations. What is wanted in such a written or spoken record is a factual account of whatever it is he chooses to record about. In the early stages of learning to do this he must choose a beginning and an end, although he will be aware of happenings which have effected the beginning and that it is unlikely that the process ends where he chooses. Having selected an 'incident' or part of a group's total interaction, he writes this down as fact, rather like the policeman giving evidence in court, free of opinion and emotive language but including his own feelings and actions. As far as possible he attaches names to the members involved and records conversation in as much detail as he is able or at least giving indications of who said what and how it was received. Such detail avoids the generalized comments 'a good discussion followed' which tells little of individual's feelings or contributions, 'most members agreed' which says nothing about the process of agreeing and who dissented. Putting names to those involved helps him to reflect on each person, on his role in the group, his part in the particular 'incident'.

Example: 'Tom's gang arrived in their usual belligerent manner and commandeered the billiard table, threatening anyone who tried to get a game. They do nothing else in the club and are extremely troublesome.' This may be written by the worker in a less emotive manner and containing more information as 'Tom, Mick, Barry and John form a tight friendship group, usually arriving and leaving together. Tonight they occupied the billiard table and resisted other members who tried to get a game on the table. Billiards and snooker seem to be their sole activity in the club and they have little communication with the other members.'

As the 'incident' is written originally it tends towards the negative and the language used seems to reflect more the worker's feelings of inadequacy to offer any constructive help or reflection on why these members behave in this way. In the second account the 'case' is stated less emotively, less judgemental and is more likely to lead to reflection of a positive nature. The former is less likely to improve the worker's knowledge or service to the group, than the latter, simply in the way it is written. There is a pre-judging in the original recording which precludes any observation of movement and change possible within Tom's group and a danger of stereotyping these members so that their behaviour will be interpreted to fit in with the expectation of the worker.

Reflection – Analysis of the Recording

When the worker writes down some factual account of something he has observed he will need to reflect on this and to analyse it. The written word here is used to remind him of what happened and to discipline his thinking. He will bring to this reflective and analytical process all that he knows about the agency's purpose, methods of work, the particular young people, his knowledge of human behaviour, group processes and his own awareness.

Examples

1. Diane arrived at the club earlier than usual. When told that the friendly netball match had been called off by the opposing team she threw her kit on the floor, and began to shout abuse at the other club, me and everybody else remotely connected with the club. She threatened to resign as secretary and dashed into the cloakroom. Returning about four or five minutes later she cut short my attempts at explanation with a near apology. She said she had had a row with her mother because her tea had not been ready when she returned from work. Other members had now arrived and Diane moved away from me to join them.

Reflection: Diane is seventeen and has been a member for three years. She has just been made secretary of the netball team. She has a number of friends in the club but is not universally popular and only average as a netball player, but is a good organizer. How far do the rest of the girls in the team 'use' her because of her organizing ability? This was to be the first game she had organized, and she may feel she would lose face because it was not to take place – through no fault of hers. How can she be helped to take this sort of let-down? Ignore her threat of resignation – not intended anyway – but does she want me to plead with her not to resign? I know her mother goes out to work as well. Was her request for an early tea a reasonable one? In what sort of mood did she leave home? Is she aware of her mother's feelings? Can the netball group help Diane?

2. Alan, John, Bill, Terry and Harry appear to use their seniority to monopolize the two table-tennis tables. They seldom play games but indulge in long 'knock-ups'. Tonight a number of younger members complained. When I asked Alan and Co. to use one table and allow other members to use the other table, Alan replied 'These nippers are a nuisance' and 'They have not got passed the ping-pong stage'. I restricted Alan and Co. to the one table, freeing the other for the younger members. I noticed the older members taking action against the younger ones and the latter 'baiting' Alan's group.

Reflection: Could I have handled this in a way which would not have resulted in appearing to take sides? The young members took advantage of my intervention. Alan was obviously annoyed at my intervention. He is a good player but somewhat intolerant. Bill and Terry are more amenable and may be helpful in coaching the younger ones. Where do they stand in their group? Alan is dominating this activity group but appears to be dodging responsibility. He refused to stand for office in recent elections. Says he has 'a thing about rules' but makes his own! How does the members' committee figure in this? If they handle it, it will almost certainly mean stricter rules governing the use of the tables? Not sure that I would like that, but would it be in the club's best interest to let them handle it and the possible consequences?

3. Miss J. informed me that Christine was annoyed about the netball game – not the cancellation, but because she had not been at the selection meeting and had been moved from her 'best position as shooter' and because Hazel had been dropped from the team. Miss J. had said she could not comment because she was unaware of what had happened, but would find out.

Reflection: Christine knew of the selection meeting but had a 'prior engagement' – the committee was not sorry! Christine is unpopular, a good player but overbearing. She picks her own position and I suspect the girls moved her deliberately. I must explain to Christine that the selection committee has the right to move people. Must explain to both committee and Christine that such moves should be the result of consultation. Do I tell Christine about the impression she gives? I suspect the group took advantage of Christine's absence from the selection meeting to move her to demonstrate their feelings towards her. Not informing her, except through the team-sheet on the notice board, was avoiding a face-to-face confrontation with Christine. Does this incident have any bearing on Diane's 'explosion' early in the evening? She was to play in Hazel's place. There is a lot of conflict in this group, and I must find ways of helping the individual and sub-group problems. Miss J. may be helpful here but it is unfair to expect her to handle it at the moment after only three months in the club. She is sensitive to the personality conflicts in the group and is showing caution in not being used by the different factions.

4. Bryn and Tony again operating the record-player.

Reflection: This is becoming a mini-discotheque each evening. Bryn and Tony have provided a second turn-table, lighting effects and prepared their own slides. The choice of records is in their hands, in fact, most records are their own. This has become almost their sole activity in the club. At the moment the response to what they do is good and they provide a useful service. The interest seems more than a passing 'fad'. My intervention has been almost nil except to say that if they require assistance in any way to let me know.

5. Mr. L. complained that he had trouble with Jim who was a nuisance in the pottery group. This evening he had 'fooled about' and upset other members of the group – he had splashed water on other members and flicked pieces of wet clay at items waiting to be put in the kiln.

Reflection: The small pottery group is progressing well and Mr. L. is a good instructor. The group is a friendship group and Jim does not fit in. He tends to float from one activity area, never settling to do any work but obstructs others. He has no obvious friends in the club and is becoming a bit of a scapegoat. I know little about his background and he is a difficult person to engage in conversation. Jim must be kept out of the group, at least until he shows some change in attitude. I must devote more time to him.

Selection in Recording

The worker in the complex club situation cannot record everything that happens and needs to make a selection of group activity, individual behaviour and events to focus his reflective and analytical attention. The selection should not depend on the dramatic incident or trouble-areas only but include the 'ordinary and normal' happenings in the club. Through such records and the interpretation and analysis he is enabled to see and understand the kind of relationships being established in small groups, the effect of the adult members of his staff and the kind of problems being encountered by groups and staff in meeting needs and pursuing programme. He becomes aware, through this process, of what he knows about individuals and groups and also of gaps in his knowledge and understanding. As he continues to record and reflect he can, over time, look at every aspect of his role, see every person in relation to the small groups and the club, question the structure of the club in terms of its assistance or hindrance in the development of people and through this make some evaluation of the progress of individuals and groups. Although the worker selects what he will record he uses his previous experiences to add to the reflective process. Some of this has been stored in memory and not written down, but the more he uses the recording method the less he relies on memory when making evaluations about people. He is also able to trace or connect situations over a longer period of time which helps in his understanding of behaviour.

Method of Recording

There is no one way of recording and each worker will develop his own style. The records shown earlier demonstrate a way of thinking rather than a method to be followed. However, a number of factors are important, some have been indicated already.

First, because our work is concerned with understanding and helping individual persons as they work together in groups, we write about individual behaviour in relationship to the group situation. This means naming people and bringing into our thinking *all* we know about the individuals: their position in the group in terms of likes and dislikes; the things that irritate as well as please others; what they bring to the group in terms of skill, prestige, status.

Second, we write about the participation of each member of the group situation; what they offer in action, how this is received or rejected by others.

Third, we record the part played by the worker or other staff member in his helping role: the action he takes and how this is perceived by individuals and groups: what he feels about individuals and groups and what action he needs to take as he progresses with individuals and groups.

Fourth, we record the relationship between individuals, groups and the formal structure of the club and agency: the clarity of purpose, or lack of it: its change to meet new situations is reflected by the growth of the group.

In the examples of recording there are two distinct parts, the first the actual event and the second the result of the reflection. In the second part the worker has included previous knowledge and understanding to help him interpret a particular piece of behaviour. He has also reflected on what needs to be done, mostly in the form of questions or alternatives. Some of the action suggested by the reflective process is administrative, some is dependent on gaining more knowledge and some action may be a conscious decision not to intervene (Bryn and Tony and the mini-discotheque), at the moment.

This may be restated as: the process, the reflection and the ensuing action. How it is written or recorded is a matter of individual preference but should contain these three elements. Many workers prefer to use all the elements in one piece of writing so that the actual event or process contains the interpretation, analysis and action suggested as it goes along. If this method is used it may be useful to underline the action or make further notes on a separate sheet of paper as an *aide-mémoire*.

Such records should be treated as confidential matter and how and where they are kept is of paramount importance. From time to time the worker should go through his recorded material to analyse and summarize individual and group progress; his role in the developing process and to help in planning for the future. He will add to this what he knows and feels about the club, some of which will not be in the recordings.

Evaluation – Social Group Work Objectives

Management by objectives is a common feature of training in industry, commerce and local government and it can be useful to apply some of this thinking to the field of social work. The objectives of good social group work are seen in the effectiveness of the group as it progresses towards:

1. A degree of autonomy where the group feels a real responsibility for proposing plans for its own programme, has the opportunities to carry out the plans and is helped to

achieve objectives by the group worker who also aids the evaluation of the plan and the programme:

2. Cultural acceptance of the members of the group and a desire to help the social education of each member:

3. A democratic system which allows for conflict of opinion but encourages co-operation in formulating a diverse programme to cater for as many needs as are reflected by the members of the group:

4. A better use of resources from within the group and outside in order to advance its programme:

5. A realistic appreciation of the limitations of the agency sponsoring the group, and therefore, of its freedom within this setting:

6. Setting objectives within this but being aware of the need to relate with other groups in the community to extend the limitations or, in co-operation with them, provide other services:

7. Producing indigenous leadership with less reliance on the appointed worker for all forms of leadership.

The role of the worker in formulating objectives is less in terms of programme content in the form of prescriptions and more in seeking ways of helping the group to achieve the objectives outlined above irrespective of programme content. The content, growing out of the group's and individual needs, is important but the method of how this is made known and acted upon is probably more important, certainly equally important. If the agency and the worker are seen as offering external (that is external to the group) expertise such expertise can only be really effective if the group itself is desirous of change, that is change in the way it handles responsibility, planning, action and is helped to face up to the consequences of such responsibility. Real growth in social educational terms will only come when each member of the group feels a part of such decision-making and shared responsibility and realizes that there is a problem inherent in the resolving of individual, self-determination and group self-determination.

The worker can encourage the members to approach problem solving in the club by methods which will provide opportunities for growth in understanding. The problem may not always be solved to everyone's satisfaction. It may not be solved at all for it may not be the sort of problem which has a once-for-all solution, in fact, it may well be a conflict-type situation which the group has to learn to live with. Perhaps it is wiser to think of Problem-Handling rather than Problem-Solving in this context. In order to apply some discipline to problem-handling there needs to be some order in the thinking around the problem. One way is to think of it in simple steps which follow logically, for example: First – *Determine the Objective*. This may be anything from a change in a rule to a method of achieving better representation of the full club on some committee. State, preferably in writing, what it is hoped to achieve by carrying out this exercise.

Step ONE: Assemble the facts.
(*a*) What happens at the moment; what rules and customs apply.
(*b*) Get opinions and feelings of the people concerned.
Keep the objective in mind and make sure the whole story is presented.

Step TWO: Consider and Decide.
(*a*) Fit the facts together and consider their effect on each other.
(*b*) What are the present practices and policy?
(*c*) Consider possible actions and alternatives.
(*d*) Consider the effects of each one of these on individuals, groups, the agency – what are the possible reactions?
(*e*) Reach a decision.
Remember the objective. Take care that discussion has not led thinking away from the primary objective and is now dealing with a new situation. If proposed action is a 'shot in the dark' should you proceed?

Step THREE: Action.
(*a*) Who is going to take action?
(*b*) How is it to be communicated – is timing important?
(*c*) Will the announcement require reinforcement? By whom?
(*d*) Does it require agency approval?
(*e*) Will the action affect people outside the group (club)?
(*f*) If there is anticipated reaction to the decision how will this be handled? Communication is important. Who communicates,

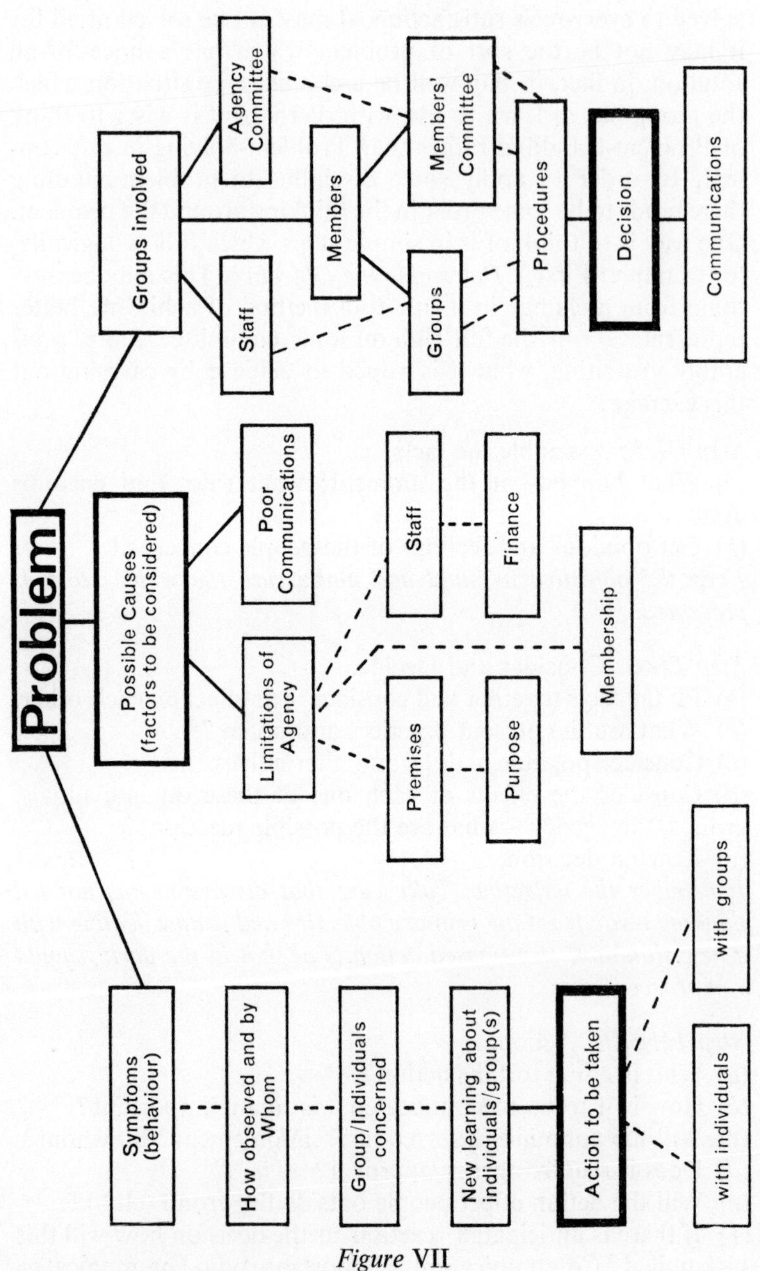
Problem
Groups involved
Agency Committee
Staff
Members
Members' Committee
Groups
Procedures
Decision
Communications
Possible Causes (factors to be considered)
Poor Communications
Limitations of Agency
Staff
Finance
Membership
Premises
Purpose
Symptoms (behaviour)
How observed and by Whom
Group/Individuals concerned
New learning about individuals/group(s)
Action to be taken
with groups
with individuals

Figure VII

how and to what groups is important. Do not dodge the issue by passing the announcement on to some other person or body, if this is necessary have a good reason for it being so.

Step FOUR: Follow-up.
(*a*) Look for reaction: how is it expressed?
(*b*) What changes are taking place in light of the decision?
(*c*) *Has the objective been achieved?*

Another approach which may be more readily used to determine a problem and to consider all the persons and groups who may be involved in creating the problem, and therefore in the handling of it, can be shown by the format in Figure VII. A format similar to this might be used in conjunction with recorded material, where the behaviour of an individual or a group may highlight a problem which can only be handled fully when all the other areas or spheres of influence are considered. Obviously many day-to-day recordings will deal with non-problem situations, and the left-hand column may be the only one significant at that time. However some situations will require the leader to reflect on either or both of the other columns to help him to understand the behaviour of a particular individual or group, because of a failure to recognize the limitations of the agency, poor communication between the agency and the formal structure represented by the right-hand column and the individual member or group of members. Such a format may be useful in indicating to the worker his central role in the totality of the work and the relationships and methods of work he has to adapt with different groups of people. It can certainly help him to think more clearly about responsibilities to the policy-makers in the external situation, to 'professional' colleagues and to the membership groupings.

Supervision

A further aid towards the achievement of a disciplined approach to youth work is through a scheme of supervision where a practitioner is helped to think in a disciplined way about his work by another person. No matter how well the youth worker develops a system of recording he will find this more useful when he brings his recordings regularly to another person whose task it is to help the worker's learning and to provide the opportunities for him to discuss his work in terms of goals, processes, behaviour, structure, knowledge, awareness and so on. There can be few youth workers who have not experienced certain satisfactions when they have been able to discuss their own work situation with some 'understanding person'. What they get out of such sessions may be limited in the sense of real learning but often they have a feeling of well-being because they have been able to stand-back from the night-by-night load and for a moment have become somewhat objective. There seems to be little doubt that one reaches a level of objectivity when discussing one's work with another person that is difficult to achieve alone.

Only in recent years, in youth work, has there been a realization of the specific task of supervision and the skill required of a person playing this role. The development of this role is seen most clearly in case-work where supervision has the task of teaching and enabling the worker to ensure the best for the individual client through the direct worker-client relationship. In the more general field of social work, supervision is seen as a way of enabling the worker to reach a professional or disciplined use of self in the practical setting and thus to make the most of his initial and continued training. Supervision is a continuation of the learning process. Joan Tash[1] describes it as regular meetings between supervisor and supervisee for disciplined discussions based on recorded material; a relationship enabling self-learning to take place, work centred, non-authoritarian, in which the supervisee gains awareness, at his own speed. The term supervision or supervisor is used in many work settings. In most non-professional situations it carries the overtones of overseeing, checking, instructing, passing on techniques used in particular work situations and is carried out by persons of a higher rank in the hierarchy and whose main task may be to see that work is done by those lower in the hierarchy. It is, therefore, directive and aimed at the effective administration of the institution. But the purpose of professional or educational supervision is to help the practitioner further his own training. It is not to make decisions about what should or should not be done at any

[1] *Supervision in Youth Work*: Joan Tash.

stage. Therefore it is not authoritarian and the person functioning as the Supervisor is not concerned with the effective administration of the institution only in as much as he takes this into consideration when the person being supervised wants to discuss how this helps or hinders his work. At this moment in time most agencies are either reluctant or unable to find people to fulfil the role of supervisor for those full-time workers demanding such a service. However some agencies, training and professional bodies are providing training for personnel who are suitable and wish to take on this task. Whether the position will ever be reached, or desired, when all part-time workers have the opportunity to be supervised is a debatable one. However any person who has pursued a course of training, full-time or part-time, will have experienced the value of using practical situations with a course tutor and, in a way, supervision is an extension of this part of training. It is one that never ends, unlike the training syllabus, because to believe it does suggests there is a point at which all possible group situations have been experienced or some kind of prescriptions have been formulated to meet future emergencies.

Usually, in a supervisory situation, the Supervisor has the greater knowledge and experience which he uses to expand on some points for the supervisee's benefit. This knowledge and experience may not be through his work in the youth service, he may have this through other forms of work which he can make relevant to youth work. Naturally, the more he understands, or has the ability to understand, the structure and function, philosophy and sociology of the youth service the more he will be able to pose to himself a number of questions which will help him to assess the role of the youth worker(s) he will be supervising. Many youth workers like the Supervisor to see them at work and this way enhance the workers' confidence in the Supervisor. The Supervisor takes care not to let the fact that he has visited the unit of work take the place of the supervisee's recordings and interpretation. Whether he sees the supervisee at work or not he should be able to draw from him the important comments voluntarily and then discuss the implications. For instance if the worker produces a recording or recalls reactions of members where he has been involved in discussion, introducing 'new' activity, or engaged informally, the Supervisor will want to help the worker to become more aware of his relationships with individuals, how he perceives them and how he thinks the members perceive him generally and specifically related to the incident recorded. The Supervisor will be able to 'picture' the situation if the worker's recording and further explanation present the facts in the first instance and through discussion give more insights into the worker's understanding of individual and group behaviour. The task of the Supervisor is to prompt the worker to think of other interpretations as alternatives to the one he has made, not in any sense of denigrating the one made but to help the worker see why he has made a particular interpretation. Through this process further insights may be gained, the worker becomes more self-aware, he is challenged to state more clearly his objectives and to appreciate his role as a social group worker. The role of the Supervisor is not to offer solutions to problems even when faced with such questions as 'what would you have done in this situation?'

Supervision of the worker along the lines suggested, where recordings of group behaviour are used as the means to further the learning and skill of the youth worker can be broadened to include the totality of the worker's role in relation to the sponsoring agency with its possibilities and limitations. From time to time the worker will want to discuss with his supervisor, perhaps in more general terms, his total function, his own philosophy as well as that of the agency, the limitations he feels or expresses as curbs which restrict his function, lack of support real or imaginary and his concern about the worthwhileness of his work. He can be helped to apply the same understanding to these situations as to the work he does with groups of members. Through supervision he may become more realistic and recognize that there are ways of meeting or overcoming some of the limitations, recognizing that some of his feelings of frustration are more of his own making than of others because he has wrong expectations of his and their role and function and that some of them are inevitable because of the nature of the task he has undertaken.

Evaluation in Supervision

The need expressed above is a very real one, it is one of having some way of evaluating what one is doing and knowing that what one is doing is valuable and worthwhile and is perceived as such by the general public, by administrators, by those upon whom the worker and the service depends. Youth workers, like many social workers, do not feel a need to justify their work in terms of success; 'what is a successful club?' and 'how can you assess results in a youth club?' are the sort of questions posed by youth workers when facing a challenge as to the worth of their work. And they are naturally suspicious of those, often within the Youth Service, who appear to measure success or the worthwhileness of the work by the number of clients in association, the range of activity and the tangible evidence of success in trophies or awards gained. At the same time they are aware of questions, if not always asked, certainly in the minds of many outside the service, of value for money, is this something on which public money should be expended and are the methods adopted the best or the only ones which should be used. Until the youth worker can satisfy his own need to feel value in his work, not merely to justify it, but to know how to evaluate it and become articulate about purpose, method and progress towards some stated goal acceptable to the average citizen, he will continually question his role and function and have feelings of frustration or inadequacy. In an earlier chapter we talked about the intuitive way of doing things and recognized that youth workers often do what is right intuitively, but expressed a need for this to be more scientifically diagnosed and understood. The chapter on working with groups attempted to show the relationship between the process and the goal and how the group worker uses the group situation through whatever activity or programme it undertakes to move individuals towards a more positive and socially acceptable form of behaviour. This sort of progress can be measured in all sorts of terms and seen to be valuable and worthwhile by workers, clients, sponsors and the general public.

Evaluation in supervision is as important as learning or increasing the 'professional' use of self. Being able to evaluate for oneself one's own work is a highly skilled and sophisticated art and most of us require someone with whom we can establish a trusting and confidential relationship who will help us in the evaluation process. The supervisory situation will not be the *only* one in which a worker can be helped to evaluate his work, others are likely to be through in-service meetings and discussions, training sessions, public meetings, but it may be the most satisfactory one in that it is regular, disciplined and always dynamic. It has a number of other advantages in that certain criteria necessary for evaluation can be worked out, stated and accepted early in the regular supervisory sessions and whilst they have to be continually in the forefront of any discussion do not need to be fully talked through at every session. The criteria will be similar for all situations and because evaluation is a relative term the first of the criteria will be to do with purpose, aim or goal. This can be a broad definition of the purpose of youth work but will certainly need to be more specifically defined according to the agency or even the unit of work. All evaluation must be made against this aim or goal. The second will be method or how this particular agency or unit will operate in order to meet the needs of its clients. The third will be the clients themselves and further criteria will include the adult personnel of the unit and the skill required of them, the external resources which are available and the structure of the organization.

The Worker as Supervisor

Even in the most 'amicable' team of adults engaged in a youth club situation someone will be designated leader or senior worker with a responsibility for the overall business. This alone implies some sort of supervisory duty in respect of the functioning of the other members of the staff. What has already been said about supervision of the youth worker applies to him in relation to his staff and he should see himself playing this role in order to help them gain from supervisory sessions. The degree to which he takes such sessions will depend on the role of the particular helpers. There may well be a different approach in intensity and frequency of sessions with the helper in the coffee bar as with the pottery instructor and different again with the assistant leaders. The starting point here is the defined role and function of the particular member of the staff, but in all the different roles and functions the leader has a responsibility to help them feel more effective in their work. With some of his staff, those who operate like him, using their social group work skill, he should encourage the use of recorded material and the regular supervision session. There are a number of ways of doing this. Some leaders expect members of staff to complete a 'nightly report sheet' with details of the groups they have worked with and individuals they are concerned about; others have introduced a 'general report sheet' on which any member of staff can record a case, individual or group. Such records have to be followed up by the leader if any benefit is to be had, and time seems to militate against this. Perhaps the most satisfactory way is to adopt the recording process outlined earlier but, again, the staff members will expect this to be handled regularly if it is to be seen as having value.

Staff discussions are of course invaluable and if the two-fold purpose of organization and supervision can be recognized even if not always separated the staff will feel benefit from discussing 'cases'. Groups often bring to light more information than is held by any one member of the staff and a relationship with a particular member of staff that has not been realized by the staff as a whole or the particular worker who has been focusing his attention on the case being discussed. It also has the advantage of giving each other a better picture of individual case-loads and passing on information which all staff members should have. The leader helps the staff to understand why confidentiality must be respected and in this way encourages them in the handling of their 'case-load'.

Whatever methods are adopted are time consuming and youth work is a very practical occupation. One can always be doing something with a group of members. But time expended on reflection, discussion and evaluation can be more profitable in the long run in terms of meeting clients' needs and more effective use of skill by adults engaged in the work and therefore of greater satisfaction for all concerned.

Appendix 'A'

CHRONOLOGICAL TABLE

Development of the Youth Service seen in a chronological sequence alongside a selection of historical factors having some relation to the study of young people from 1780 onwards.

1780		Sunday School Movement – root from which sprang our system of day schools (Robert Raikes).
1790		Day school opened in Southwark by British & Foreign Schools Society (Lancaster): 'all who will may send their children and have them educated freely': monitor system and rotary scheme – advanced pupils teaching beginners and one teacher controlling large school.
1802		Health and Morals of Apprentices Bill.
1807		Whitbread's Parochial Schools Bill, on behalf of the pauper children, rejected.
1811		First Voluntary School Building Association (Free Churches) National Association formed by Church of England (Bell) – National Schools leading to the Dual system.
1820		Lord Brougham's 'better education of the Poor' Bill rejected.
1823		First Mechanics Institute founded.
1833		Althorp's Act to regulate the labour of children and young people in mills and factories. A motion before Parliament calling for universal and national education was withdrawn, but the first Government grant (£20,000) for education was made.

1834		Poor Law Commission to look into the working of Poor Law, provision of relief, eradicate pauperism.
1839		Government Grant for Education increased to £30,000: half-time schools; pupil-teacher system.
1840		First state official appointed: special committee of the Privy Council appointed.
1842		Mines Act prohibited child and female labour: boys under 10 not to be employed.
1844	Formation of Y.M.C.A. – 'concern for the spiritual welfare of young men in drapery and other trades by the introduction of religious services among them'.	Factory Act: working day for children not to be longer than 6½ hours: women and young persons 12 hours between 5.30 a.m. and 8 p.m.
1845		Number of voluntary teacher training colleges had increased to 22.
1846		Secularists (Lovett & Ellis) set up first Birbeck School in Holborn and included in the syllabus psychology, social science, natural history, drawing, music, besides the normal 3 R's, but excluding the teaching of doctrine or religious instruction. Committee of Privy Council extended aid to teachers other than in Church inspected Training Colleges
1850		Act to establish half-day holiday in some jobs. Factory Act – 60 hour week.
1851		Octavia Hill – pioneer of good working-class accommodation.

1853	Formation of Y.W.C.A.	
1856	Formation of Prayer Union.	
1861	Formation of Association for Girls	Newcastle Commission revealed no real diffusion of elementary education among poor classes: thousands of parishes without schools.
1859–69		Robert Lowe followed Kay (first state official for education); introduced Revised Code; children subject to examination after first year of schooling; system of payment by results.
1870	1870 onwards. Clubs and institutes founded in Lancashire for young unemployed girls (cotton famine).	Elementary Education Act (Foster): preserved position of existing voluntary schools; gave Municipal boroughs power to make good sufficiency of premises; School Boards to be established; power to call for educational rate; secure attendance of children between 5–13 years of age.
1871		Formation of a united German state. Trade Union Act: legality given to unionism. Bank Holiday Act.
1872	Kensington Boys' Club.	
1874		Factory Act: 56 hour week.
1875	Girls' Friendly Society.	
1876		School attendance made compulsory.
1880	Y.M.C.A. *Boys'* Department established.	
1883	Boys' Brigade formed.	

Year		
1886	Hulme & Chorlton Lads' Club formed.	
1887–1900		Bournville Trust; Lever Bros. 'Port Sunlight' – Schemes of 'new-town' development.
1888	London Federation of Boys Clubs.	
1890		Housing of Working Classes Act. Local authorities empowered to build houses.
1898		Ebenezer Howard, 'Garden Cities of Tomorrow' stressed that whole freehold of garden city must be kept in public ownership for sake of planning control.
1899		School leaving age raised to 12 years.
1900		School leaving age raised to 14 years.
1902		End of Boer War; Education Act; School Boards and School attendance Committees abolished; County Councils and County Boroughs given duty of administering elementary and secondary education; development of education in its own area, according with local needs and circumstances.
1906		Education Act: local education authorities empowered to make arrangement for school meals and recover cost when parents could afford to pay.
1907	First Scout Camp. Boy Scout Movement.	Education Act: compulsory schemes of medical inspection in the local education authority schools.

1908	'Working Lads' Clubs' (Charles Russell).	
1909		'Eight Hours Act' – working day of eight hours.
1910	Girl Guides Movement.	Choice of Employment Act: local education authorities empowered to establish juvenile employment committees to offer guidance in choice of employment.
1914		Start of World War I.
1916	National and local Juvenile Organizations Committee established to concern themselves with the physical, moral welfare of the young in time of war.	
1918		End of War. Education Act (Fisher): half-time system abolished; school-leaving 14 but local authorities allowed to make bye-laws raising the leaving age to 15; education free to all regardless of income; day continuation schools to be established; local education authorities empowered to give assistance to voluntary youth organizations.
1919		Act of House and Town Planning: compulsory for urban authorities with population of 20,000 to submit schemes by January 1926 – extended in 1923 to January 1929.
1920	Young Farmers' Club formed.	
1921		Education Act: 'tidied up' a mass of heterogeneous legislation to an ordered and logical whole.
1923		Local authorities allowed to make schemes for built-up as well as underdeveloped areas 'on account

		of special architectural, historic, or artistic interest attaching to a locality'.
1925	National Association of Boys' Clubs.	Town Planning Act: Town planning established as a separate branch of legislation independent of housing.
1926		General Strike; Foundation of B.B.C.
1927		Hadow Report (Education of the Adolescent): steps to re-organize elementary education so that 11–14's not going forward to secondary schools receive secondary education in a senior department.
1929		The Great Crash.
1932		2·7 million (20 per cent of the working population) unemployed. Town and Country Planning Act extended planning powers to all built-up areas and to countryside.
1933		Hitler seized power in Germany.
1935		Restriction of Ribbon Development Act.
1936	Formation of the Standing Conference of National Voluntary Youth Organizations (S.C.N.V.Y.O.).	Education Act – school leaving age to be 15 from September 1939.
1937	Physical Training and Recreation Act; National Fitness Council.	British Medical Association's Report on the health of the nation – alarming pronouncements on the poor health and physique of the masses.
1939	Board of Education Circular 1486 'In the Service of Youth'.	World War II.
1940	Board of Education Circular 1516 'The Challenge of Youth'.	Evacuation of B.E.F. from Dunkirk.

1941	'New' Air Training Corps Scheme.	
1942	Registration of all young people, 16–18 years.	
1943	National Association of Training Corps for Girls.	
1944	Education Act.	Education (Butler) Act – new form of secondary education; community colleges; Youth Service an integral part of education.
1945	Methodist Association of Youth Clubs. McNair Report – The Supply, Recruitment, Training of Teachers and Youth Leaders.	End of World War II. Dissolution of Parliament – General election. Family Allowances Act.
1946	Outward Bound Trust.	
1948		National Insurance Scheme.
1949	Jackson Report: The Recruitment, Training and Conditions of Service for Youth Leaders and Community Centre Wardens.	
1951	Fletcher Report: The Recruitment and Training of Youth Leaders & Community Centre Wardens.	General Election. Cut of 5 per cent in expenditure by Local Education Authorities.
1954		Ministry of Food abolished.
1955	Citizens of Tomorrow – report published by King George Jubilee Trust.	General Election.
1956	Duke of Edinburgh Award Scheme launched.	Restrictions imposed on credit, hire purchase and capital issues.
1958	'Albemarle' Committee appointed.	

1959		General Election.
1960	Albemarle Committee Report 'The Youth Service in England and Wales'; Youth Service Building Programme; National College for the Training of Youth Leaders; Youth Service Development Council; Optional course in Youth leadership in eleven Teacher Training Colleges.	
1961	'Youth Service' – monthly broadsheet published by Ministry of Education. Joint Negotiating Committee for Youth Leaders – Youth Service Association.	
1962	Bessey Report on Training of part-time leaders.	Teacher Training Courses extended to three years.
1963	Newsom Report 'Half our Future'; Robbins Report on Higher Education.	
1964	Youth Service Information Centre, Life of National College for the Training of Youth Leaders extended to 1970–71.	Ministry of Education became Department of Education & Science. General Election. Industrial Training Acts.
1965		Sports Council appointed to advise on the development of amateur sport and physical recreation; to foster co-operation between statutory and voluntary organizations.
1966	Boy Scouts Association 'Advance Party Report'. Girl Guides Working Party Report on the future of the Organization.	

1968	Community Suggestions (later to be Innovations) Centre founded.	Age of Majority lowered to 18.
1969	'Youth and Community Work in the 70s.'	Report–Y.S. Development Council
1970	National College for the Training of Youth Leaders closed; three additional two-year courses in Youth and Community work training – Goldsmith's College, London; College of Education, Leicester; John Dalton College, Manchester. N.A.B.C. and Y.M.C.A. Courses extended to two years. Westhill College of Education Two-year Course.	General Election.
1971	Y.M.C.A. Commission Report.	

Appendix 'B'

Guide To Further Reading

HISTORY OF THE YOUTH SERVICE

Brew, J. Macalister — *Youth and Youth Groups* – a framework for youth-work; selected chapters on historical development of youth movements.

Eager, W. M. — *Making Men* – the history of boys' clubs and related movements in Great Britain.

Evans, W. — *Young People in Society* – origins and early development.

Gibbon, F. P. — *William A. Smith of the Boys' Brigade* – the story of the founder.

Haycocks, N. — *Voluntary Organizations in the Youth Service.*

Hubery, D. S. — *Emancipation of Youth* – the needs of young people in nineteenth and twentieth centuries; religious and uniformed organizations in the Church.

Percival, A. — *Youth will be led* – the story of the voluntary youth organizations.

Reynolds, E. E. — Baden-Powell – story of the beginnings of the Boy Scout movement.

Russell, C. E. — *Lads' clubs* – working-class lads' clubs.

Williams, J. — *The Life of Sir George Williams* – story of the beginning of the Y.M.C.A.

ADOLESCENCE

Bedford, R. — *The World of Young People* – earlier maturity; new prosperity; new freedom; questing for standards; searching for a faith.

Fleming, C. M. — *Adolescence* – psychological and physiological growth; the adolescent at home, school, work; threshold of maturity.

Hanmer, J. — *Girls at Leisure* – a report based on London and the Home Counties in 1962 and 1963; needs and interests of girls; use of their leisure.

Hemming, J. — *Adolescents and Society* – the growth tasks of the adolescent; conflict between adult and adolescent thinking.

Hemming, J. — *Problems of Adolescent Girls* – an analysis of 3,000 letters received by weekly periodicals.

Musgrove, F. — *Youth and the Social Order* – the myth of adolescence; Society's creation of an adolescent period; disadvantages and advantages of segregational adolescent age-groups.

Odlum, D. — *Journey Through Adolescence* – physiological and emotional change.

Wall, W. D. — *Guidance in Adolescence*: development related to behaviour; adolescent tasks; relating to new situations.

WORK WITH YOUNG PEOPLE

Goetschious & Tash — *Working with Unattached Youth* – a teaching document of case histories; making a Christian commitment relevant to the needs of contemporary youth work.

Goldman, R. — *Angry Adolescents* – factual story of voluntary leader and a club started for young people in a Home Counties village.

Gosling, R. — *Lady Albemarle's Boys*: experience of self-programming group; problems of freedom.

Morse, M. — *The Unattached* – 3 year project carried out by N.A.Y.C.; contacting; talking; attitudes; role of detached workers.

Parieth, M. — *Branch Street* – leisure pursuits of a slum gang.

Spencer — *Stress and Release in an Urban Estate*: Bristol Social Project on family and neighbourhood in a developing community.

Turner, M. C. — *Ship Without Sails* – Barge experiment; Mutiny order; attitudes of adult crew and locals.

GROUP WORK

Homans, G. C. — *The Human Group* – the small group, primary groups and their significance to the socialization process; behaviour in groups.

Klein, J. — *The Study of Groups* – structure; assumptions; organization, development of a 'culture'; communications.

Matthews, J. E. — *Working with Youth Groups* – Social group work skill; the function of the Youth Leader; disciplined approach.

Milson, F. — *Social group work Method and Christian Education* – leadership functions in the Youth Service; group dynamics; Christian leadership.

Olmsted, M. S. — *The Small Group* – the study of groups; group behaviour; the sociology of groups.

Sprott, W. J. H. — *Human Groups:* the primary group, relationships, roles; crowds and other collections of people.

COMMUNITY WORK AND STUDIES OF COMMUNITIES

Benedict, R. — *Patterns of Culture* – study of three primitive societies; custom, norms; diversity of cultures.

Biddle and Biddle	*The Community Development Process* – principles, ethics, skills, analysis.
Goetschius, G.	*Working with Community Groups* – helping autonomous Community groups in their work of offering recreation and social welfare services to their members.
Leaper, R.	*Community Work* – common ground explored in an experimental course.
Ross, M. G.	*Case histories in Community Organization.*
Thomason, G. F.	*The Professional Approach to Community Work* – community development, community organization, content and method goals, strategies, self-help.
Young and Willmott	*Family and Kinship in East London* – a study based on Bethnal Green, 1953–55 and new housing estate in Essex; effects of re-housing in family life.

ADOLESCENCE IN FICTION

Barstow, S.	*A Kind of Loving* – story of a young man and his move to adulthood; infatuation, love, influence of home.
Braithwaite, A.	*To Sir with Love* – coloured teacher in the East End: discipline, illiteracy, delinquency, promiscuity, affection, love, respect.
Brooks, J.	*Jampot Smith* – middle teens experiences in war-time Llandudno; friendships, courtships and struggles with 'rights' and 'wrongs'.
Golding, W.	*Lord of the Flies* – schoolboys stranded in an uninhabited island without adults; breakdown of society; groups, relationships, barbarism.
McInnes, C.	*Absolute Beginners* – teenagers and their outward show and inner feelings; racial tension.
Sillitoe, A.	*The Loneliness of the Long Distance Runner* – a boy in Borstal; authority, isolation.

For Further Consideration

The following questions are suggested for the use of groups or individuals using this book as a textbook for study.

Chapter One

Has the development of a Youth Service helped or hindered the integration of young people to the community as a whole?

What stable features can be discerned throughout the changes in approach and policy in youth work?

Is the 'voluntary' principle an outdated concept?

To what extent is statutory action appropriate to social education and leisure?

Why is training necessary for a part-time worker?

Chapter Two

What difference does the existence of a Youth Service make to your youth work situation?

Is free and equal partnership compatible with grant aid and statutory provision?

How can Local Education Authorities, voluntary organizations and youth workers effectively co-operate in the service of youth?

Chapter Three

How can you learn to understand someone whose experience is very different from you own?

Is socialization a liberating or a conditioning process?

What are the distinctive contributions and temptations of male and female workers in relation to adolescents.

What are the major influences on your own decision making?

Chapter Four

What do you think are the characteristics of a 'responsible' person?

By what right and method do you attempt to discern the needs of other persons?

What do you regard as the ideal relationship between a school and a youth group in the same community?

In what ways can the part-time youth worker relate to other community workers with young people?

Chapter Five

What sanctions must a youth worker accept in order to be effective in community work?

Are beliefs and convictions an asset or an embarrassment to a youth worker?

Why are the ethical concepts of Acceptance, Self-determination and Confidentiality binding for you?

How is the principle of confidentiality to be practised in a team of youth workers?

At what point do the purposes of sponsoring agencies conflict with the purpose of youth work as defined here?

Chapter Six

Is the cultivation of an 'esprit de corps' compatible with the needs and aspirations of individuals?

What links are desirable between a youth group and other groups in the same Church or Community?

What degree of self-government is practicable for a youth group?

How would you set about dealing with a disruptive group or gang which has infiltrated or invaded your youth work situation?

Chapter Seven

What are the dangers of wanting to help people?

Is pastoral care compatible with counselling?

To what kind of person would you turn for counselling?

Chapter Eight

How are values expressed through programme?

Should all youth groups be self-programming?

What kind of programme planning is consistent with flexibility and responsiveness to situations?

How can young people be helped to analyse and evaluate programme for themselves?

Chapter Nine

To what extent should members be involved in management of youth work?

How important is efficiency in administration?

To whom is the youth worker accountable?

Why is it important for a youth worker to be able to work with adults?

Chapter Ten

What influence does the worker's attitude to the Law have upon the young people with whom he works?

What limitations does the legal responsibility of the youth worker place upon the principle of self-determination?

How should the youth worker deal with infringements of the law, e.g. under-age drinking, gambling, drug-taking.

Chapter Eleven

What recording is essential for effective part-time youth work?

How can a part-time worker obtain supervision?

What determines the objectives of a youth group?

By what means can a qualified youth worker continue to learn and grow?

Appendix A

What connections if any do you discern between stages in the development of youth work and other historical factors?

Appendix B

How can you obtain access to a wide range of literature relating to youth work?

INDEX